ENGLISH LEAVES

MASTER DAY,
SON OF SIR JOHN DAY, WITH HIS CRICKET BAT
From the Painting by George Romney

ENGLISH LEAVES

BY

EDWARD VERRALL LUCAS

Essay Index Reprint Series

BOOKS FOR LIBRARIES PRESS
FREEPORT, NEW YORK

First Published 1933
Reprinted 1969

STANDARD BOOK NUMBER:
8369-1361-2

LIBRARY OF CONGRESS CATALOG CARD NUMBER:
73-99709

PRINTED IN THE UNITED STATES OF AMERICA

TO
BERNARD DARWIN

CONTENTS

LIST OF ILLUSTRATIONS

ix

ENGLISH LEAVES

THE MOTHER OF ENGLAND

IT is odd that the oldest road in England—and, for many miles on both sides of London, the straightest—should bear a no more distinguished and resonant description than Watling Street; nor are the authorities very sure why it is called that. Some Saxon of importance may have led the Romans, who made it to join up Dover (Dubrae), Canterbury (Durovernum), London (Londinium), St. Albans (Verulamium), and Wroxeter (Viroconium), to give it his name. All that is known is that it was first called Waeclinga, or Waetlinga, Street, and to this day nothing more imposing or more suggestive of our austere conquerors has been invented.

Although so many centuries have passed since Watling Street was constructed, and motor-cars have replaced the long series of horse-drawn vehicles that rumbled over it, this highway is still the best road for a traveller from London to Canterbury. Down Watling Street went the Roman soldiers in their clanking armour; down Watling Street went

the Canterbury Pilgrims; down Watling Street went
Henry VIII to meet the Emperor Charles V; down
Watling Street go we: at any rate, as far as Harble-
down, where the view of Canterbury opens and
the sublime central tower of the cathedral is seen
rising serenely and majestically over the trees and
roofs.

All the while we are in Canterbury we shall be
conscious of this glorious dominating structure with
its four pinnacles: seen from every distant point
and, as we circumambulate, seen, expectedly or
unexpectedly, at the end of so many streets. It is
the slender spire which usually carries the extreme
suggestion of height, but I think that, in time, one
comes to associate this central square tower of
Canterbury Cathedral with the maximum.

Watling Street on its way from London swerves
at Harbledown only as a highway; the old track
still goes on, keeping the line down the hill to the
Stour. This river it crosses twice, the little island
of Binnewith having to be negotiated, and when
in the city you will see the precise spot where the
Roman ferry was, marked by a tablet claiming it
as the actual birthplace of the 'Mother of England'
—as Canterbury proudly calls herself. Close by is
the house of a dyer who states roundly, though not
so poetically, and I am sure justly, that his hand
and that of his predecessors have been continuously

CANTERBURY CATHEDRAL FROM THE SOUTH-WEST

'subdued to what they have worked in' since the year 1189.

Such boasts are of the essence of Canterbury, where the word 'old' has a different connotation from that of most towns which specialize in it, having, indeed, no need at all of the final 'e' which apparently is found so irresistible by the tourist. When, in moving about this storied, inexhaustible little England of ours, we see a sign with 'Ye Olde' on it—Ye Olde anything, even almost Ye Olde Noveltye Shoppe—the period thus glanced at is rarely earlier than Tudor; but Canterbury's bricks are largely Roman. No need for such an artifice as a final 'e' there.

Should, very wisely in good weather, the traveller prefer to approach Canterbury on foot, he ought, for old time's sake, to forget Watling Street and make use of a section of the Pilgrims' Way, on which the devout or the anxious, or both, coming from Winchester to find comfort for their souls at the Shrine of St. Thomas Becket, were wont to set their determined feet. The Way runs west and east, south of Watling Street, and the modern pilgrim from London wishing to end his journey in the mediaeval manner would probably join the track near, say, Maidstone, climbing the hill at Thornham (where the Kentish cricketing Colossus, Alfred Mynn, is buried) and keeping under the ridge, past Hollingbourne and Charing and Challock and Godmersham Park and Chilham Castle, to Harble-down, where the Way and Watling Street become one. It is probable that to-day, when the old, simple, spontaneous and unpretentious exercise known as walking has been dramatized into 'hiking' and has become a cult, the Pilgrims' Way is again crowded.

The mention of Roman bricks is a reminder that Kent, of which Canterbury is the heart and the jewel, was twice invaded, and twice conquered, by the Romans, and the second conquest (with modi-fications) still holds. First came, in A.D. 43, the Pagan army of fighting men with swords and spears and catapults, led by Aulus Plautius, one of Claudius's generals, to capture the eastern districts and begin a colonization which lasted for three centuries, and many traces of which—not the least being Watling Street—endure to this day.

'Everybody', said the late Archbishop Temple, in an address of welcome to the American Ambas-sador a few years ago, 'visits Canterbury twice'; and so with the Romans, for in A.D. 597, also landing in Kent and making Canterbury a stronghold, they came again; but this time they were soldiers of the Cross under Augustine, to reinforce our Christianity.

Every one knows the Venerable Bede's story of Pope Gregory I, when Abbot of St. Andrew's in

Rome, seeing in the slave market in the Forum some foreign youths of fair aspect, and indulging in that ecstasy of punning which was to lead to this missionary effort.

'Where do they come from?' he asked.

'They are Angles,' was the reply.

'Not Angles, but angels,' said the abbot. 'They have the faces of angels and should be co-heirs with them in heaven. What is their province?'

'Deira.'

'De-ira? Truly they shall be saved from the wrath of God and called to His mercy. What is the name of their king?'

'Ælla.'

'Then must Alleluia be sung in Ælla's land'; and forthwith he vowed to visit England and convert it wholly to the new faith. Illness, however, prevented, but when he became Pope Gregory he quickly arranged for Augustine's mission.

It must not be thought that Augustine was the first bearer of the news of Christ. Very far from it. There is the early legend of Joseph of Arimathea at Glastonbury in the first century A.D. While in the year 314, or nearly three hundred years before Augustine's landing, Britain was sufficiently Christian in religion for three of her Bishops to take part in the Synod of Arles—the Bishop of York, the Bishop of London and the Bishop of

Lincoln—all intent on making new rules for the well-being and greater solidarity of the Church. If there was no representative from Canterbury, it was because Kent had not yet come in. Before Augustine's landing there, however, in 597, a little spade-work had already been done, for although Ethelbert, who was then King of Kent, and his people were true to the old British gods, his queen, Bertha, a Frenchwoman, was a Christian. Ethelbert seems, however, to have had an open mind, for when the news came that Augustine's pacific party had disembarked in Thanet, he summoned his counsellors and met the missionaries in person, very prudently sitting in the open air lest they cast spells over him; and on hearing their message of peace on earth and goodwill to men, he took a chance and offered to make them comfortable at Canterbury, although he could not promise anything on behalf of his subjects generally.

Ethelbert himself was soon baptized, and you may see to this day the font beside which he stood for the sprinkling, for it is preserved in the little church of St. Martin, on the hill to the east of the city: the church which, transformed from a Roman temple, the King had given to Bertha for her own use.

Since St. Martin's is not only the first Christian church in the country but also one of the oldest in

Europe, the visitor to Canterbury who wishes to
be orderly in his study of the city should, having
trod the stones of Watling Street, begin there; from
which, having heard the confidential old lady mur-
mur the story of its long and memorable past, and
having admired the fair prospect of the cathedral
framed between two yew-trees, he should pass on
to the ruins of St. Augustine's Abbey; for this
establishment was the first organized religious institution in the country. The Abbey was based upon
the royal palace which Ethelbert, a very thorough
convert, gave to Augustine for a home for himself
and his monks, adding his own private temple,
which they quickly consecrated as the church of
St. Pancras, and in which, under the sky as a roof,
you may still stand. Although little now remains
but walls and foundations, there are reconstruction
charts to help the imagination towards visualizing
the scene of ecclesiastical activity which these grass-
covered undulations represent.

On the spring day that I was last there yellow
wallflowers sprang with equal gaiety and sweetness
from Saxon, Roman and Norman crannies, while
the twentieth century asserted itself in the shape
of a motor lawn-mower preparing the cricket ground
which now covers the sites of refectories, dormitories,
brew-houses, hospitals, and all the other accessories
of a great religious house, now hidden beneath the
2

turf; for the monastery founded by Augustine at the end of the sixth century became, in the nineteenth, a college for missionaries; and young dispensers of the Gospel need their recreations as much as the non-elect. Just as the Roman cleric came here with his followers in 597 to convert England, so are these youths going out into the far places to spread the same tidings to the heathen; and, for all I know, to start new Canterburies on alien soil. Meanwhile, on this spring afternoon a great many of them were following the dictates of a sensible, if not conspicuously theological, French commentator on life, and were cultivating the garden.

It was in 601 that Augustine received from Pope Gregory his authorization as head of the English Church, and the next year he decided upon Canterbury as his see, and, when he died, he was buried here in his own abbey, where King Ethelbert and Queen Bertha also lie. His Saint's Day is May 26th.

Although the situation of St. Augustine's grave is not certain, there are in Canterbury two of his relics that can be both seen and touched: in the cathedral his throne, in which all Primates since have sat for their formal induction, and in the Museum the wooden chair, crude but substantial, occupied by him at the second Synod of British

CANTERBURY
THE GOLDEN BOOK OF THE BUFFS

Bishops in 603. If there is in existence in England a chair older than this, I have not seen it.

The history of Canterbury Cathedral between its earliest days and the tragic event of 1170 which transformed it into a shrine and place of pilgrimage needs a volume for the telling. Let us for the moment forget the Danes and their atrocities of 1011, and the Normans and their rebuilding, and come to the reign of Henry II and the afternoon of Tuesday, December 29th, when the archbishop of that day, Thomas Becket, was hacked to pieces. The criminals were four knights in armour: Hugh de Moreville, William de Tracy, Reginald Fitzurse, and Richard le Breton, purporting to be carrying out the will of Henry, who, absent in France, had, in their hearing, peevishly demanded: 'Who will rid me of this pestilent priest?'

The floor of the north-west transept, where the crime was committed, is still the same, and a stone marks the actual spot, but the neighbouring stairs of Becket's day have been built in. The murder caused consternation throughout Christendom, and Henry had no peace of mind until he had made some effort at expiation, by submitting himself, half-naked, to be flogged by priests at his victim's tomb. I hope they laid it on.

Becket was canonized as St. Thomas of Canterbury in 1173, his day being December 29th, and

in 1220 his remains were reburied beneath a shrine
behind the high altar in what is now called St.
Thomas's Chapel, and the Canterbury pilgrimage
became increasingly popular and the gifts increasingly valuable.   Henry the Eighth, however, who
in 1520 had humbly prayed here in company with
the Emperor Charles the Fifth, in 1538 publicly
degraded the saint and deprived the shrine of its
jewels.   The body was again interred, this time in
the crypt: but whether or not beneath the slab
that one sees is not known.   I feel it possible to
say with more certitude that it is unlikely that the
damp stain on this slab can be directly ascribed to
Henry II's tears, and even more unlikely that the
faint adumbration of a human figure on a neighbouring pillar, photographs and picture-postcards
of which are sold in the thousand-and-one souvenir
shops in Canterbury, is, as it is claimed to be,
Becket's ghost.

The beauty and grandeur of Canterbury Cathedral are not to be communicated by words.   As
they make a special appeal to each of us, the visitor
to the city should grasp at every opportunity of
being in the building and in the Close, which is
one of the quietest in all our cathedral cities, steeped
in placidity and lately made even more sacred by
the Kentish War Memorial walled garden.   Here,
amid the lulling discord of jackdaws and rooks,

one may realize something of the spirit of Chaucer's own England, for there are no backwaters like cathedral Closes. All the residences suggest leisure and comfort, but they are not conspicuous architecturally, not even the palace where the Primate lays his head. It is for the cathedral vistas that one lingers here, and not least, in my own case, for occasional soothing glimpses of the long leaden roof of the choir, with its gracious grey hue and delicate ornamentation.

Every inch of the cathedral inside and out is wonderful, not the least exquisite of its beauties being the little circular (and secular) water tower on the north side, a gem of Norman design. There is enough to occupy the visitor for weeks, from the earliest Roman vestiges in the crypt, which began probably as a temple in honour of the old personal gods, and the tomb of Edward the Black Prince, with his coat of mail, his gauntlets and his shield over it, to the Golden Book of the Buffs in St. Michael's Chapel, a leaf of which is every morning ceremonially turned by a soldier who arrives from the barracks for that pious purpose. Reconstructive work is always in progress, the little chapel of St. Edward, where two priests used constantly to say masses for the soul of Becket, being the latest addition, now a refuge for those who would meditate or pray.

One thinks of the cathedral as Canterbury's chief
glory; and of course it is, although St. Augustine's
Abbey has, in a way, more importance; but Canterbury, as a whole, is what they call in France a
ville musée. And all Canterbury is interesting,
almost every building having had some previous
historic existence—there is a pastrycook's, for
instance, in the High Street, which once lodged
Queen Elizabeth—and every alley or gateway, as
you will find if you are curious enough, leading to
some ancient structure, modernized, perhaps, but
authentic underneath and still beautiful in parts.
Never was such a jumble of past and present. As
one example I would cite the charming river journey
—almost Venetian in character—to be made from
the Black Friars' monastery on the banks of a branch
of the Stour, in which, after its dissolution, Crom-
well stabled his horses, and in which, later still,
the Unitarians had their place of meeting—to the
Huguenot weavers' hall, with its gables and diamond
panes; and then through the bridge under the High
Street, with motor-cars and char-à-bancs rumbling
above you, to what remains of the Grey Friars'
monastery on the Island of Binnewith of which I
have already spoken: a retired abode of peace built
over the stream, in the midst of gardens and the
song of birds.   No one knows Canterbury who has
not made this almost secret excursion.

Then there is the need to ascend the mound called Dane John on the wall of the city, from which the cathedral seems to be more unreal and lovely than from almost any other point, and where, when I was there last, two very proud peacocks and six less ostentatious peahens were strutting about the grass. And for another embracive view of cathedral and city there is the roof of the tower of the West Gate, at which Canterbury is entered by all travellers from London, where a collection of arms and armour and instruments of correction is preserved, among them a scold's mask, which the custodian, a smiling old cynic, thinks should never have become obsolete.

This noble gate, by the way, was very nearly destroyed in quite recent times through as odd a chance as could be devised even by a fertile professional humorist. In fact, I would wager a larger sum of money than I could afford against the cause of its momentary peril being guessed. But this is what happened. Canterbury, somewhen in Victorian days, was being visited by Wombwell's Menagerie, advancing upon the city from the north, and when the elephants arrived at the West Gate—this was at a time when all the vehicles had to pass through it—it was too small for them. Mr. Wombwell therefore, with the arrogance of the successful showman, demanded nothing less than that he should be rid of this pestilent portal. And such was the desire of many of the Town Councillors, hastily convened, to have the wild beasts in their midst, that removed it would have been but for the casting vote of his Worship the Mayor.

As I have remarked in a companion essay on Winchester, the West Gate in that city, a very similar structure to this, but never, so far as I know, menaced by a monstrous pachyderm, has a similar collection of weapons.

Canterbury has also its representative civic Museum, with pictures and plans of Canterbury from earliest times, and objects dug from the earth belonging to times still earlier, before pictures and plans were made, including Roman earthenware and Roman bronze, some of it far more comely than anything made to-day, and improved rather than impaired by centuries in the engentling earth. Here also is a collection of the tokens which Pilgrims bought and carried away with them to ensure their well-being during life and after it, and I noticed, in celebration of the Kent as we know it to-day, with its oasts and clustered poles, a bust of 'The Hop Queen', by a modern sculptor, fairer far than the carved head of the historic Fair Maid of Kent (as the spouse of the Black Prince was called, although when she married him she was a widow with three

CANTERBURY
THE WEAVERS' HALL ON THE STOUR

children), which you see on a boss in the chapel bearing her lord's name: the chapel where the French Protestant weavers still worship.

Canterbury's purely literary associations begin with Chaucer, who sent his pilgrims there from the Tabard in Southwark, telling their tales by the way. The city itself was merely their destination, but its name is none the less imperishably united to that of the father of English poetry, upon whom Mr. Chesterton recently wrote such a humane and exhilarating book. Canterbury's latest literary association is with Joseph Conrad, the second Conrad in her history, the first being Prior Conrad, in the twelfth century, the builder of 'the glorious choir' beneath whose roof Becket was slain. Canterbury claims Joseph Conrad as a son for the reason that, having ceased to be a sailor, he retired to Kent and is buried in the Roman Catholic section of the Whitstable Road Cemetery, with these lines from Spenser's 'Faerie Queene' on his grave:

'Sleep after Toyle, Port after stormie seas,
Ease after Warre, Death after Life, doth greatly please.'

The last time I saw Conrad was in Canterbury in the St. Lawrence Ground, during a Canterbury Week. He was on a coach, watching the cricket through an amused and slightly perplexed, if not contemptuous, eyeglass. I climbed beside him and did what I could to make things clearer, but his interest was in the whole situation rather than in technique.

Between Geoffrey Chaucer, who died in 1400, and Conrad, or Joseph Teador Konrad Korzeniowski, who died in 1924, the brochure bearing upon Canterbury and literature which lies before me takes note of three other writers. The first is Christopher Marlowe, the dramatist, who was born here, in a house in George Street, in the same year as Shakespeare, 1564, and died in a stabbing affray at Deptford in 1593; and whose glorious extravagant pen gave us the play of *Tamburlaine the Great*. The monument to Marlowe, which used to be just outside the entrance to the Cathedral Close, but has been moved to the Dane John Park, was unveiled by Sir Henry Irving in 1891, nearly three hundred years late. The dominating figure is the muse of Dramatic Poetry; the four little bronzes on the pedestal represent Irving as Tamburlaine, Sir Johnston Forbes-Robertson as Faustus, James K. Hackett as Edward II, and Edward Alleyn, a contemporary of Marlowe, as the Jew of Malta.

The third author on the list, Daniel Defoe, has but the slenderest claim to be there, having been little more than a visitor; but the fourth was as thorough a Man of Kent and son of Canterbury as could be imagined, with wit and humour added: Richard Harris Barham, first a rural clergyman and later Canon of St. Paul's, known to the world as 'Thomas Ingoldsby', a genial antiquary and go-as-you-please poet upon whom Holy Orders exercised no undue restraint. Not only was Barham born in Kent (at 61, Burgate, Canterbury, in 1788,) and brought up there, but his first curacy was at Ashford and his second at Westwell; while his last Kentish home, before he left for London in 1821, was at Snargate on the edge of Romney Marsh, where smuggling was still an industry. You could not well be more Kentish than that.

Barham did not begin the *Ingoldsby Legends*, which are saturated with Kentish lore, until he was forty-eight, 'The Spectre of Tappington' being the first of the first series. References to Canterbury are constant in them, while one, 'Nell Cook', is a reconstruction of a local tradition concerning the Dark Entry leading to the Cathedral from the King's School playground. The story is told by Master Tom Ingoldsby, a King's schoolboy himself, who, it will be remembered, was such a long time in telling it that when he returned he was well caned for being late—and nothing could give the muse of Barham more pleasure than such a calamity as that.

It has before been remarked, with satisfaction,

that in a world where injustice is rife, Heaven, oddly enough, has arranged that the originator is often the best; and such is so in the case of Barham. Countless imitators have attempted the *laissez-faire* Ingoldsby tradition, but no pupil has excelled the master, which means, of course, that to write like Barham one has to be Barham. Such a mixture of fun, fancy, recklessness, historical and ecclesiastical knowledge, intimacy with current events and skill in rhyme cannot be assembled either by the wish or by prayer and fasting. Every amateur, especially the young—for I look upon Barham as pre-eminently a schoolboy's poet—must have attempted his style. I remember with blushes an effort of my own; but the professionals tried, too. I can recall a book written in collaboration by Frank Smedley (the author of stories in prose which were to me in those distant days as glorious as the *Ingoldsby Legends* in verse) and Edmund Yates, called *Mirth and Metre*, which attempted to reap in the Tappington fields, but gathered a very indifferent harvest.

My present copy of the *Legends* is dated 1882, the Edinburgh edition (why Edinburgh, I wonder? for there is nothing less Scotch than this book), with added illustrations by Tenniel and Du Maurier, some of Tenniel's very good; but this is not the edition in which I read first, and learned from, for that was long before 1882. I had, before I was in the teens, the whole of 'The Execution' and 'Misadventures at Margate' by heart, and so many lines from the others that when I re-read them the other day I found my memory often leaping in advance of the text. 'The Jackdaw of Rheims' and 'The Knight and the Lady' hardly needed to be read at all. How jolly they are and how well-preserved! Many of the allusions are now obscure; some of the humour looks old; the digressions can be tiresome; but, apart from the ingenious rhyming, there is an exuberance, a gaiety, a don't-care-a-rappishness, and a profound common sense that keep them vital.

A strangely belated tablet was put upon Barham's birthplace in Burgate, now a lawyer's office, two or three years ago and unveiled by another man of God and dignitary of St. Paul's, who in his writings is as little like 'Thomas Ingoldsby' as may be— Dean Inge.

And here, having mentioned the Dark Entry, let me say that King's School, to which it leads from the Cathedral, or from which the Cathedral is gained by the scholars, is one of the oldest schools in England, refounded in 1541 by Henry VIII, who otherwise has not much to his credit in this city; and hence its name: Henry was the 'King'. Its special architectural treasure is the Norman staircase, which no one visiting Canterbury should miss.

Lovers of Dickens will be pleased, when in Canterbury, to see in what piety the fame and name of that great man are held—and all on the strength of *David Copperfield*, for he was never more than a visitor to the city (when he put up at the Fleur de Lys), and had no early associations with the place, as he had with Rochester. It is a real tribute to his genius as a creator of men and women to see the local habitations which have been found for the figments of his brain, some of them hastily engendered probably on the spur of the moment, yet more actual to his readers than most of the people we know or even our familiar relations: even those we call—and they are always the most Dickensian—Uncle and Aunt. It was almost a shock to me to see in the souvenir shops picture-postcards of the house of Agnes Wickfield and her father, and of Uriah Heep's 'umble 'ome: authentic structures of brick and wood and stone which can be visited to this day—the Wickfields', for instance, in St. Dunstan's Street—for, vivid as their imaginary inhabitants are, they still were fictional, or so one had supposed. Yet now that I have seen the photographs I have my doubts. For the camera cannot lie, can it?

Whether we want these picture-postcards is

another matter.   When a house has been described like this, as the Wickfields' was: 'At length we stopped before a very old house bulging out over the road: a house with long, low, lattice windows bulging out still farther, and beams with carved heads on the ends bulging out, too, so that I fancied the whole house was leaning forward trying to see who was passing on the narrow pavement below' —when, as I say, a house is described like that, no one needs the photograph of an actual building which may or may not have been in the author's mind.   The writer who could invent Mr. Wickfield at his port, and Agnes Wickfield with her chatelaine keys, and Uriah Heep at his desk, did not need to see an actual building in which to environ them.

When, however, we come to the Sun Inn in Mersey Lane and find that it claims to be one with 'the little inn' where Mrs. Micawber told David about Mr. Micawber's misadventures with the Plymouth branch of the family, the book is, so to speak, extra-illustrated in the right way.   For inns are different.   'It is truly painful to contemplate mankind in such an aspect, Master Copperfield, but our reception was decidedly cool.   There is no doubt about it.   In fact, that branch of my family which is settled in Plymouth became quite personal to Mr. Micawber before we had been

there a week. Under such circumstances', she
continued, 'what could a man of Mr. Micawber's
spirit do? But one obvious course was left. To
borrow of that branch of my family the money to
return to London, and to return at any sacrifice.'
Mr. Wickfield may not have lived at 71, St. Dunstan
Street, but I feel convinced that those inimitable
words were spoken in a private room in the Sun.
Inns, as I have said, are different from houses.
It could easily be proved, by a little research, that
no tenant named Wickfield had ever occupied 71,
St. Dunstan Street; but few know who has stayed
at inns and no one knows who has casually drunk
there.

That was on the occasion of Mr. Micawber's
first visit to Canterbury, after having investigated
the possibilities of the Medway coal trade, and
it is significant that when he returned thither to
be the confidential clerk of Messrs. Wickfield and
Heep he referred to it as his 'native heath'. 'We
came', said Mrs. Micawber, 'and saw the Medway.
My opinion of the coal trade on that river is that
it may require talent, but that it certainly requires
capital. Talent, Mr. Micawber has; capital, Mr.
Micawber has not. . . . Being so near here, Mr.
Micawber was of opinion that it would be rash
not to come on and see the Cathedral. Firstly, on
account of its being so well worth seeing; and,

secondly, on account of the great probability of something turning up in a cathedral town.' All this was spoken in 'the little inn', where, later, it will be remembered, David joined Mr. and Mrs. Micawber at dinner, and later still—in fact, a quarter of an hour after that festive evening was finished—Mr. Micawber wrote the letter beginning, 'The die is cast—all is over.' Surely it is all to the good that when seeing the Sun Inn at Canterbury we should think of these things, and when reading these things we should think of the Sun Inn at Canterbury.

Among the prints relating to the history of the city, in the Canterbury Museum, is an engraving of the Canterbury Catch Club in 1826: a large company of convivialists at table, each with a church-warden pipe, or yard of clay, and a tankard or a wine-glass or a spirit rummer before him, and the motto 'Harmony: Unanimity' on the ceiling above. The names of these jovial whiskered fellows are provided in a key, all of them save two earning their living, the president being Mr. Charles Delmar, brewer, and the two exceptional members without any low traffic with toil being Mr. Marseille, gentleman, and Mr. Hollingbury, gentleman. If the name of Mr. Wickfield, lawyer, is not here it is because, I feel sure, he joined later than 1826. 'Harmony: Unanimity'—what a club to ask Mr.

3

Micawber to, as a guest! and how rejoicingly he
would have added to his letter of reply, accepting
the invitation, the hope that he might bring with
him his son Wilkins, who, it will be recalled, had
a remarkable head-voice, and was, indeed, destined
by his father for the Church by way of the cathedral
choir. He would probably have added that Wilkins's repertory consisted chiefly of the songs of
the 'immortal exciseman nurtured beyond the
Tweed'.

Lastly it is interesting to remember that Izaak
Walton's marriage, in 1626, to Rachel Floud, was
celebrated in St. Mildred's Church. But there
are other great men besides those who write books,
and I never go to Canterbury without visiting St.
Gregory's churchyard, for there you may see Fuller
Pilch's grave, with a very graceful bronze relief
of the old master at the wicket, most happily recon-
structed from the drawing of him, under the title
'The Batsman', which George Frederick Watts as
a young and struggling artist made for Pilch's and
Mynn's friend and Kentish colleague, N. Felix.
The monument is a little way on the right as you
approach the west door of the church: a column
rising from a square base, with inscriptions on the
north and south surfaces which run thus—on the
north, 'Fuller Pilch, born at Horningcroft, Norfolk,
March 17, 1803, died at Canterbury, May 1,

1870, aged 67 years'; and on the south, 'This monument was erected to the memory of Fuller Pilch by upwards of two hundred friends to mark their admiration of his skill as a cricketer and his worth as a man.'

That so beautiful a city has been much painted need not be said; but only one illustrious artist is associated filially with Canterbury; and he is illustrious no more, for times have changed and highly polished kine are out of date. I refer to Thomas Sidney Cooper, R.A., one of the most popular exhibitors at Burlington House summer after summer for an incredible number of years, whose scenes of cattle reclining in the lush meadows beside the Stour were the desire of every Victorian collector. Cooper was identified with Canterbury all his life. He was born there in 1803; he lived there; he died just outside, at Harbledown, in 1902; and he endowed the city with an art school, where, I take it, his sister the cow is honoured as she should be.

ENGLAND'S ANCIENT CAPITAL

W E saw when we were at Durovernum—or should I say Canterbury?—that, after landing in Kent in A.D. 43, the Romans consolidated themselves and then made their road, Watling Street, to Wroxeter, gradually subduing and annexing the rest of England and apportioning it among provincial governors. A site so eminently fitted for a military centre as Winchester, with its surrounding rampart of hills and Southampton Water so near, was quickly discerned, and therefore Winchester, or Venta Belgarum, was founded as the meeting-point of six roads, not the least populous of which led to and from the seaports of Bittern and Porchester; while another ran through Atrebatum, or Silchester, to London, or Londinium, the Thames, or Tamsa, being crossed at Pontes, or Staines. These Roman roads, although they were made eighteen or nineteen centuries ago, are still our approaches to Winchester, from whatever point we come.

Before the Roman conquest Winchester had been important—such is the testimony of the revealing

spade—as a Celtic stronghold. After the Romans
faded away, weary of stubborn colonization and
homesick for Italian sun and wine, it was important
again as the capital of the kings of Wessex, who
later were to rule all England, of whom the first,
Egbert, was buried here in 839, while in the old
painted chests set on the walls of the cathedral choir
is the *débris* of a whole dynasty. For centuries Winchester was the London of England. Alfred ruled
here; Canute is buried here, also his queen, Emma,
founder of the religious institution whose name is
preserved in the very old house known as 'God
begot' in the High Street, now a tea-shop; Edward
the Confessor was crowned here; William the Conqueror made it one of his homes, to be near the New
Forest glades and coverts; William II was buried
here; Henry VIII feasted the Emperor Charles V
here; Mary was married here to Philip of Spain.

It was Charles the Second's intention to have
a country palace here, and Sir Christopher Wren
was instructed to draw up the plans; but though
the plans were made and are in existence, the
building was only begun and has since been incor-
porated in the barracks in the Southampton Road.
Other links between Winchester and the second
Charles are Nell Gwynn and Prebendary Ken.
In 1683 the Merry Monarch's merry mistress,
chancing to pass that way, demanded the use of

the prebendal house during her visit, but Ken, although he was one of the King's chaplains, stoutly refused, saying that a woman of ill repute had no place under a clergyman's roof. It is all to the credit of Charles that when, a little later, the bishopric of Bath and Wells became vacant, he should have insisted upon its being given to 'the little black fellow who refused his lodging to poor Nell'.

We saw when we were at Canterbury how the second Roman invaders, bringing Christianity, established themselves there at the end of the sixth century. To Winchester, where there was, almost beyond doubt, a pagan Roman temple, now lost in the foundations of the cathedral, the new religion in due course came, the Roman missionaries landing on the shore of Southampton Water and the first bishopric being founded in 662. Of Winchester's earliest ecclesiastics there is no room here to speak, but it is noteworthy that in the ninth century the Bishop was St. Swithin—not, of course, canonized until later—as a matter of fact, on July 15th, 971 —and St. Swithin was a prelate and organizer of great piety and good sense. He was counsellor to Egbert, and tutor to the heir to the throne, Ethelwulf; as an historian he was probably the originator of the 'Anglo-Saxon Chronicle'; he was a builder, among his works being a bridge over the Itchen. As a performer of miracles he shone both during his life and after it. Should a woman carrying eggs over his new bridge chance to fall and break them, what did the Bishop but make them whole again? while his tomb was a resort of all who were poor in heart or body. Among his most lusty devotees was a hunchback whose hump his magical beneficence had removed.

If to-day, when miracles at his shrine are no longer expected, St. Swithin is known more as a weather portent than as a man of God, it is no fault of his. The origin of the superstition which makes July 15th so critical to the young and the athletic (for whom the sun chiefly shines) is the legend that when the time came, on July 15th, 1093, for the saint's translation from his chapel outside the cathedral to a resting-place within, there was continuous rain for forty days, until, in fact, interpreting the deluge as a mark of his disapproval, the monks desisted. The only tangible memorial of St. Swithin that is left is the iron grille which once protected his shrine from the too passionate pilgrims and which has now been set up before a doorway in the cathedral's north-west nave.

St. Swithin may be the best known of Winchester's bishops, although not in his episcopal capacity, but he had followers of more importance to the present structure; notably the first Norman bishop, Walkelyn, a cousin of William the Conqueror, who was responsible for the magnificent Norman work in the transepts and the first nave. The tower which he built at the west end collapsed in 1107, as a sign, it was thought, of divine displeasure due to the burial of so impious a king as William Rufus in this spiritual and sacred place. The tower was never rebuilt in its old position, but set in the midst, where it now is. Walkelyn's cathedral, begun in 1079, was finished by Bishop Henry of Blois, King Stephen's brother, a century later. It was then that the black font of Tournai marble, which you now see in the nave, was installed, with its carvings of scenes from the life of the children's patron, St. Nicholas.

At that time the bishops lived, not, as to-day, in a quiet gentlemanly residence, hard by the cathedral walls, surrounded by flowers and trees, but in a fortress to the south-east of the cathedral, built by Henry of Blois and known as Wolseley Castle, within whose ruined walls lawn tennis is now played. You find it at the far end of College Street.

For the cathedral nave as we now see it, with its stone-vaulted roof, we are indebted to the most potent of all the long roll of Winchester's bishops, William of Wykeham, who founded the school and gave it its famous motto, founded New College, Oxford, and was Chancellor of England under

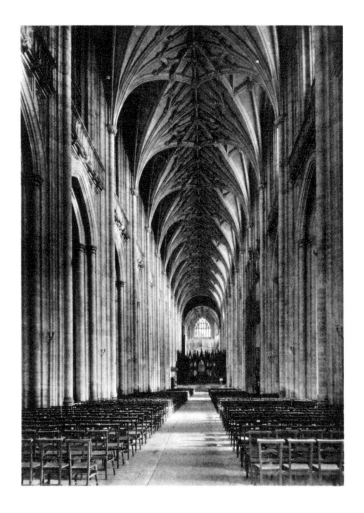

WINCHESTER CATHEDRAL
THE NAVE

Edward III and Richard II. Bishop William of Wykeham was educated at Winchester, he administered the see for thirty-six years, and in 1404 he was buried in the chantry which bears his name.

If it is possible, you should always enter a cathedral by the west door, which at Winchester is open whenever the weather permits. The eye thus receives a shock of pleasure more sudden and memorable than any subsequent impression. Particularly is this the case at Winchester, where the roof of the nave is unbroken to the far, far end, and where the external solidity of the building has not prepared you for such mystical whiteness and grace.

Of detail there is too much to see for any pen to be able to cope with, from, say, the Chapel of the Holy Sepulchre, the earliest of the Gothic accretions, with its primitive paintings, to the recent and very pompous tomb of Bishop Samuel Wilberforce, so different from the simplicity of Bishop Fox's, with its humble *memento mori* beneath. The cathedral is, one might say without exaggeration, inexhaustible, and I envy those who have time to study it and absorb it.

Among the lay tombs not the least appealing is that of Izaak Walton, who died here in 1683, aged ninety. His slab, in the floor of Prior Silkstede's chapel, was inscribed by 'the little black fellow', Bishop Ken, who was half-brother to Walton's second wife, Anne Ken; his host, in the close, was Bishop Morley, who held the see for twenty-two years and was a good friend not only to the church and state and to the compleat angler, but to Winchester itself, for it was he who built and endowed the college for matrons, named after him. In addition to Walton's tomb, the cathedral has a statue of him, and, in the Silkstede chapel, a fisherman's window, where, in the lowest lights, right and left, the good old man is seen, once by the Itchen, meditating over a book, and once, by the Dove in Derbyshire, in company with Master Charles Cotton, his collaborator.

Another literary shrine in Winchester Cathedral is that of the author of *Pride and Prejudice*. Although Winchester is proud to claim Jane Austen as a citizen, she came here, alas! only to die, with her slender golden tale of work never to be resumed. She arrived in May, 1817, to be near a famous physician, taking lodgings in College Street, in the house where a tablet has been placed, opposite a beautiful quiet walled garden, and in July she died. But her grave, in the north aisle of the nave, has made Winchester a place of pilgrimage. The inscription, while drawing attention to 'the benevolence of her heart, the sweetness of her temper and the extraordinary endowment of her mind', says nothing of the men and women whom she created and added to our own domestic circles: not even the Rev. William Collins is mentioned.   O rare Jane Austen!

The Winchester cathedral Close has not the order of Canterbury's or Salisbury's, and it seems to be peculiarly the haunt of cyclists; but show me any Close without some distinguished reserved English residence, some vistas of herbaceous border, some stretches of green turf, and a sky speckled by daws.   The haunts of ancient peace in these feverish times of house-planning and arterial roads belong chiefly to the clergy, who prove themselves worthy inhabitants.

Having referred to Salisbury, let me say that there could not well be two cathedrals so unlike as Salisbury and Winchester: not only in style, but for the reason that one of them is never lost to view and the other is rarely to be seen from any distant spot.   Wherever you are, in Salisbury, or in the surrounding country, the cathedral spire visibly pierces the sky.   But Winchester's low central tower, in its hollow amid the hills, sinks into secrecy. You fail to find it even from the school playing-fields; even from St. Cross, across the meadows. St. Catherine's crown of windswept trees might be said to do for Winchester what the spire does for Salisbury; catching sight of the clump, we say 'There's Winchester'.

Winchester, though pre-eminently ecclesiastic and scholastic, is yet instantaneously in touch with some of the wildest country in southern England. A city entirely surrounded by game, with, on its ramparting chalk hills covered with the soft fragrant turf, an invigorating aromatic air which to Keats, seeking health for his poor inadequate lungs, was worth 'sixpence a pint'. Parts of its old wall remain, just outside which, on the west, is the castle where Alfred the Great held his parliament and where to-day justice is administered. The noble hall, built with supreme massiveness, has been beautified and dignified by the addition of the statue of Queen Victoria by Sir Alfred Gilbert, wherein you may recognize the same hand, but firmer, that recently gave London the Queen Alexandra Memorial, with the same quality of sensitive bronze. Above it hangs a circular wooden disc, painted in sections, which for some foolish reason it is customary to describe (and to photograph) as King Arthur's Round Table, but which could not accommodate the company and is certainly not more than five hundred years old and probably much less. If you open the little south door of this Great Hall you will find a few vestiges of the palace which Sir Christopher Wren began for Charles II.

Another modern sculpture in this city is in the

WINCHESTER
THE CLOSE

Close, by Mr. John Tweed—the figure of a soldier in a simple natural posture who stands for all his comrades in the King's Rifle Corps who perished.

I am not in a position to state whether Canterbury turned the upper part of her West Gate into a museum before Winchester did, or whether Winchester's West Gate took the lead; but the similarity of the two portals and their possessions is very peculiar. Both serve as entrances; both specialize in the machinery of punishment and in old armour; both invite you to the roof for a view of the city. Winchester has an iron framework used for hanging in chains; hooks for pulling thatch off burning houses; a most malignant man-trap, and one of the jack-boots which Charles II left at the Deanery after a visit there. The West Gate is at the top of Winchester's narrow High Street; at the foot, just by the glorious statue of Alfred the Great, is another museum, where you may see the birds of Hampshire stuffed and set in their natural surroundings, and a group of nests of small inoffensive twitterers on whom that impudent non-householder, the cuckoo, has imposed an egg.

Alfred the Great while at Winchester supervised the first history of the English people in the English tongue—the *English Chronicles*. His wife Ealswith founded the Abbey which stood, close to the statue, where the public gardens now are. A manuscript prayer book used by the first Abbess as long ago as the ninth century may be seen in the British Museum. Thus is time bridged!

The similarity of the two West Gate museums is not the only reason for thinking of Canterbury while one is at Winchester. They have an actual link, or line of communication, which still exists, as old as the thirteenth century. We saw at Canterbury the stone that marks the spot where the shrine of Thomas Becket was placed, the objective of every traveller along the Pilgrims' Way. It was at Winchester that the Way started. No doubt the devout, foot-sore but hopeful, were to be seen plodding towards Canterbury every day of the year, but the two great formal Pilgrimages, comparable to the processions to Lourdes at the present time, contemplated reaching Canterbury either on or before December 29th, the anniversary of the murder of the saint, or on July 7th, the anniversary of his translation. The Way ran from Winchester to Alresford, Ropley, and Farnham, where the Bishops of Winchester had a Palace, and so on across Surrey and Kent.

In writing of Canterbury I said that to recommend her antiquity she was in no need of assistance from the alluring word 'olde'. Nor is Winchester; but Winchester has succumbed to the temptation. I found both 'Ye Olde Booke Shoppe' and next to

'Ye Olde Brasse Shoppe' with Winchester's various devices—such as the symbol of St. Cross and the famous Trusty Servant in the school—reproduced as metal souvenirs.

It is between these aggressively ancient establishments and the entrance to the Close that the little Winchester Museum is situated, the custodian of which is one of the most willing and best-informed men who was ever put in charge of Roman remains. Not merely Roman: Saxon and Norman and mediaeval, and all indigenous, and some of the oldest and most interesting of them unearthed recently by the workmen digging foundations for the new Woolworth building in the High Street. Thus do the ages meet. Among the Woolworth *trouvailles* is a Saxon hand-mill, or quern, made of an upper and a nether stone. In one of the glass cases is a Norman leaden treasure-vessel which, when found, contained six thousand silver coins of the reigns of the Conqueror and his son, the theory being that it was buried in order that that son, the predatory and avaricious Rufus, might not sequester them. Two of the coins are shown; rather like pretty sixpences of our own day. Here, too, is a section of one of the beech trunks forming the cathedral foundations at the end of the twelfth century; here is a section of mosaic pavement from the old Roman palace where Little Minster Street

now stands, a narrow thoroughfare to-day given over
to garages.   And, coming nearer our hearts and
bosoms, here are a bead bag and a bead purse and
a needle-case which once belonged to Jane Austen.

But although downstairs there is no exhibit
which the custodian does not lovingly demonstrate,
it is upstairs that he longs to lead you, because of
the remarkable collection of flint implements and
weapons which he himself arranged and can enlarge
upon in the liveliest manner.   The history of mankind, for two hundred thousand years, is in this
room.   A staggering apartment; and it is well to
bring oneself back to simpler emotions by looking
at the specimens of Hampshire wild flowers which
are renewed every few days; among them the fly
orchis and the spider orchis and other miracles of
the chalk.

Winchester is not such a meeting-place of the
waters as Salisbury, but under the old bridge at
the foot of the High Street gurgles the speedy
Itchen, beside which, for a while, you can walk
on your way to St. Cross and perhaps see a king-
fisher as you go.   If you would read of this river
as the abode of trout and the home of pleasant
memories, as they can be set down only by an old
Wykehamist who reverences his school, you should
obtain a copy of *Fly Fishing*, by Lord Grey of Fallo-
don—a book that has the right to stand on the shelf

reserved for the best writers on the open air, from
Walton to W. H. Hudson.

St. Cross is the square church on the right, across
the bright grass, and the charity of St. Cross is one of
the oldest in England, a country rich in such
endowments. Within its walls live thirteen
brethren, in, I trust, amity; some of them, those
in the mulberry uniform, coming from the uni-
versities, and the others, those in black, from the
rank and file of life. Every one is marked by the
silver cruciform emblem. St. Cross also feeds
many poor people every day, and any wayfarer
wishing for a piece of bread and a tankard of beer
may have it for the asking. I had some myself.
The place, which dates from the twelfth century,
is a refuge indeed, and, on my last visit, sitting
outside one of the residences while church service
was in progress, and smoking a pipe in the hot
sun, I realized that, were enough votes given me,
I could very naturally subside into the brotherhood.
There is yet time.

After church I joined a party that was being
convoyed round the premises—three visitors from
the north of England and two Americans—and
we saw all the show pieces and were told their
history. Not least interesting to me was the rude
and, I should guess, painfully uncomfortable, chair
in which William of Wykeham, one of the con-

4

trollers of St. Cross, used to sit; and resting my hand on the arm I hoped that a finer courtesy and more consideration for others might one day be mine. Should there be any choice of guides, my advice is that you ask for the services of John Turner, a brother of eighty-four, with a certain humour of his own. He had been, he said, a London pastrycook before he had the good fortune to be selected as an inmate here, and in his rooms, to which he led us, I saw his likeness, taken when he was a vigorous man of middle age, with the photograph of one of his confectionery masterpieces beside him; and in a glass case was the plaster-of-Paris symbolism which he had once designed for a christening cake. On another wall I noticed a reproduction of Millais' 'Boyhood of Raleigh', but there was no sign of 'To-morrow will be Friday', by Dendy Sadler, which ought to have been there because it was at St. Cross that it was painted.

Winchester is a pleasant city with kindly people in it, and in the cathedral is the most impressive white nave I have ever seen, and in the midst of the school cloisters, that gem, the chantry, one of the most exquisite little buildings I have ever seen; but I came away from my last visit almost wishing I had never been there. I had been walking about the school; I had rejoiced in the little isolated chantry; I had sat in the chapel and let all the rich

colours of the great window gladden the eyes; I
had loitered admiringly and reverently in the
cloisters recently built by Sir Herbert Baker as a
War Memorial—perfect in their scheme and design
and material; and then I strolled on to the playing-
fields and watched several cricket matches at once
and again marvelled how often it happens that the
bowlers do not coincide in their attack, so that one
can see first one batsman squaring up to the ball
and then another.

It was a fine afternoon, and there were anglers
in the distance by the Itchen, and fleecy clouds
intensified the blue over St. Catherine's Hill.
Strangers are treated with the courtesy of inattention
in this place, where the motto 'Manners makyth
man' was first applied, and I was permitted to sit
in front of the pavilion as though it were my right.
In course of time there came to the same seat one
whom I knew to be a master because hats were
doffed to him. 'Were you at school here?' after a
while he asked me. Never have I said No with
more reluctance and regret.

GREENWICH OBSERVATORY

THE English have done many odd things, but none more strange than to surrender, apparently, all control over new buildings, and particularly when these are factories and works. But for such incomprehensible laxity, how could those huge chimneys have been permitted to soar along the riverside at Greenwich to thicken the atmosphere in which the Royal Observatory has its being? This was the question which I asked myself as I stood the other day on the Observatory roof, and, looking west, instead of seeing St. Paul's rising over the Tower Bridge, was confronted by a murky veil. It is of very small importance, it is true, whether a tripper to Greenwich, like myself, can see or not see, but it is vital to the trained and vigilant eye seeking to ascertain the movements of stars.

Before Charles the Second, thinking chiefly of his sailors at sea and their astral needs, directed Sir Christopher Wren to build the Observatory in Greenwich Park, the Tower of London had been our astronomical headquarters, although the

Queen's Palace at Greenwich, down by the river, was also used. The first Astronomer Royal was John Flamsteed, who gives his name to the residential part of Wren's building, where, the other day, two little boys were performing skilfully on a vehicle of which neither Wren nor his most ingenious contemporary, Sir Isaac Newton, who often visited here, ever dreamt: the bicycle. Flamsteed, who was a chronic invalid always working under difficulties, came into residence in 1676, with a salary of £90 a year net, and the task of instructing two Christ's Hospital boys added to his official duties. The instruments provided were utterly inadequate, and, in order to buy more at his own cost, he took a number of paying pupils. The story of his conflict with red tape, with jealous and unimaginative scientific men, with poverty, with ill-health, and with Newton (upon whose sun his dealings with Flamsteed are the only spot), is a miserable one; but he never despaired, and his labours in mapping the heavens were invaluable.

Wren's portrait and Flamsteed's portrait will be found in Wren's octagon room, from which, looking down the steep grass slopes, you have spread out before you beside the Thames the white hospital buildings designed by the same lavish hand. He refused any fee for his services. When asked what he should be paid, his sole reply was 'Let

me have some share in an act of charity and mercy.'
Noticing the fine new statue on the terrace beside
the Observatory, I naturally assumed it to be either
of Flamsteed or some other watcher of the skies
or of the great London architect himself; but no:
it was that of General Wolfe, a gift from Canada,
the famous soldier's association with Greenwich
being the presence of his remains brought from
Quebec to the parish church. Thus Kent has two
statues of this romantic warrior (the other being
at Westerham, his birthplace), and none of the first
Astronomer Royal.

Astronomers I have always thought of with a
mingling of respect and fear and a great wonder.
Only a very brave or very insensitive man, I have
fancied, could traffic with the immensities of the
heavens and the uncountable and belittling stars,
so many of them vastly more significant than that
on which we dwell. But now that I have been
to Greenwich Observatory I have still another
feeling for these researchers, and that is admiration for their hardiness; for they can work only at
night, the roof must be open, and the telescope
rooms may not be heated. To lose the blessed
hours of the day is privation enough; and then to
be chilled all night! No, I shall stick to the pen.

Flamsteed's prevailing handicap, rheumatism,
contracted while at school, could not but be aggra-

vated by his studies; and it is interesting in these
days, when massage and osteopathy are fashionable,
to remember that he was one of the unsuccessful
patients of the famous Valentine Greatrakes, the
Irish 'stroker'.   Flamsteed was an exception, for
Greatrakes, by his manipulations, cured hundreds
of sufferers, chiefly of scrofula but also of ague
and gout.   At first his patients had to go to him in
Ireland; but later he moved to Lincoln's Inn Fields,
exercising his gift, which he believed to be partly
divine, equally on the poor, from whom he took
no fee, and on the rich.   He was usually triumphant,
but failed not only with Flamsteed, whom he
'stroked' in vain, but at Whitehall, where some
illustrious invalids had been assembled to be dealt
with as test cases in the presence of the King and
Queen.

   I left till the end what I had chiefly in mind when
I decided at last to see the Observatory: the meridian
of Greenwich.   I wanted to stand on the spot where
this imaginary but important line springs away to
the north and the south on its Puck-like journey
round the world.   A very easy thing to do, I found
it, for there is a little gate with a notice directing
one to it, just by the twenty-four-hour clock whose
second-hand remorselessly and wastefully ticks away
our brief span.   Two schoolgirls entered immediately before me, full of excitement.   'I've often

heard of it,' said one, 'but didn't know what it was.' Then, a moment later, in a voice charged with disappointment: 'What! only that line on the ground!' To me it was more interesting, for, looking south, I could fancy it making its direct and inexorable way across Kent and Surrey and Sussex—it just skirts East Grinstead, and runs right through Lewes (mingling, I have always understood, with the congregation in St. Ann's Church)—leaving the land, very sensibly, at Peacehaven, and hitting France at the little seaside town of Villers near Trouville. In its northerly course from Greenwich it crosses the west end of the Wash and the mouth of the Humber, springing away from the coast at Withernsea and just missing Flamborough Head.

A FRUGAL OLD PEER

A GOOD way to divide the world would be between those people who keep accounts and those who do not. Among the second division I most conspicuously am. For the space of eighteen months many, many years ago, I had a little notebook in which, every Sunday morning, I struggled to balance income and expenditure: a feat made possible only by recourse to the blessed word 'extras'; but never since then have I done anything but watch my counterfoils, with or without elation. And to-day, of course, we all employ the same chartered accountant: the Chancellor of the Exchequer. I know, however, men who put down every penny as it is spent and who are in an agony if anything interrupts this process and they cannot remember a transaction. In the watches of the night they endure torments of forgetfulness. Where can that sixpence have gone? Nor is it necessary for this kind of precisian to be poor. Wealth and poverty have nothing to do with the case: he keeps accounts, whether he is a millionaire or a scrivener, wholly because it is his nature to

47

do so; which is proved, I think, by the extracts from the private ledger of the third Earl of Dysart, of Ham House, near Richmond, of Helmingham in Norfolk, and of Norfolk Street, Strand, which that admirable quarterly, *The Countryman*, has recently printed.

The entries range from a halfpenny for 'Charity', a penny for sending a letter by the waterman, and three halfpence for a lemon, to £50 to 'Lady Huntingtower at her own Request to Buy Herself a Birth Day Gown', £100 'To my daughter by the Post in Bank Notes as a Present toward buying her a Pair of Diamond Ear Rings', and £360 17s. 3d. to the 'Gardiner for making ye Sunk Ditch, altering ye Parterre, and filling up ye Pond belonging to Ham House'. The years covered by the accounts are 1765 to 1770, and some of the items are very interesting as showing changes in value since that time, and exhibiting also his caprices of generosity. When his lordship stayed for the night at Ye Spread Eagle, Ingatestone, for instance, he paid for supper, lodging and breakfast, and for greasing two carriages, £1 12s. 6d., including sixpence in tips. When, however, he stayed at the Three Cups he gave the cook and chambermaid three-and-six between them.

The standard entry under the heading 'Charity' is twopence, but there were exceptions. Thus,

once 'A Dumb Woman' got sixpence, 'A Poor
Woman I met in the Park,' a shilling, and 'A poor
decay'd Farmer,' half a crown. Were the third
Lord Dysart living to-day he would, at this rate,
have few half-crowns left. 'A Pair of Stag Horns
at 4*d*. pr Pound, two shillings', has an odd sound.
The purpose was to make smelling salts, which, in
those days, when swooning was the fashion, were
more in demand than with us, whose nerves, braced
on a diet of Claxons and the franker fiction, are
equal to anything. Even more obsolete is 'A Year's
Window Tax, £2 15*s*. 6*d*.'; but we are not without
imposts of our own. 'Three Cakes of Solid Soupe,
one shilling'—who would have thought that invention so old? A Quarter of an Hundred of Pens
for one-and-threepence sounds cheap: quill pens
presumably; and a Tortoise Shell Comb for eight-
pence (before the days of celluloid imitations), and
Five Small Spunges for one and tenpence, are cheap
too, according to present-day prices; but a pound
of green tea cost his lordship sixteen shillings and
a knife a guinea. It was time he had a knife of
his own, for we find him paying 'One of ye Maids
at Bawdsey for ye Use of Her Knife', a shilling,
and 'Ye Cow Boy for ye Use of His', another
shilling. On the other hand, 'A Man at Totten-
ham who help'd to tye ye Shaft of ye Chaise being
broke' got only threepence.

Beer was not at the soaring figure it is to-day, and very possibly had more hops in it: 'To ye Job Postilion a Fort Night's Beer, seven shillings.' Another necessary fluid was cheaper, too, for one of the entries is: 'Ink, a halfpenny.' Eating-apples were sold—as they ought still to be, instead of, ridiculously, by weight—at a penny and a halfpenny each; Seville Oranges were three-halfpence each; 'Rabbets' were a shilling each; 'Colly Flowers', ninepence each. For six days' work three gardeners wanted—or received—only one pound seven, while the 'Gardiner Who found ye Dog Bango in ye King's Road and kept him a fortnight' got three and six. For an ounce of coffee, an odd amount to purchase, fivepence was paid. Dentists—at any rate, peers' dentists—were cheaper then than quite ordinary persons' dentists now are. For five false teeth his Lordship's bill was two pounds twelve and six, while both Jane and Frances had their teeth put in order for an inclusive sum of two guineas.

Frances, I take it, was one with Fanny, who is responsible for a perplexing item: 'A Driving Book for Fanny, one and six.' What was a driving book? 'An Ounce of Gascoigne Powder, sixteen shillings'—what was that for? 'To the housemaid which she found of mine, half a guinea'—what did she find? 'Three Viols of Hills Essence of Water

Dock, nine shillings'—what was that sovran against? For cleansing purposes the maligned non-bathing Continent came in useful. Thus: '2 Cakes of French Soap, one and sixpence' and 'Twelve Italian Wash Balls, half a guinea'.

Behind the accounts is the figure, shadowy but not indistinct, of a kindly patriarchal English gentleman of the irrecoverable and less complicated past, flourishing before steam, before electricity, before machinery, before gas, before petrol, before linotypes, before broadcasting, before cinemas, and, very noticeably, before trade unionism. It is very difficult for us, accustomed to all these things and to the fever and fret that they have brought with them, to set ourselves in the third Lord Dysart's place; but if the opportunity of visiting England in some past period were miraculously offered, I am not sure that the seventeen-sixties would not be my choice.

His Lordship's figures give almost no information as to what was passing at that time in the intellectual world—this selection from his accounts mentioning the purchase of only three books[1]: '*Quin's Life with Jests*, three shillings, *Daphnis and Chloe*, three pence' and '*Ye Peerage of Great Britain and Ireland*, three Vols., twelve shillings'; but we know

---

[1] As a matter of fact he bought many, as the library at Ham House testifies.

that he subscribed to *Ye Gazette*, while only two
forms of entertainment are noted: 'Four Tickets at ye
Concert, ten shillings', and 'Seeing ye Collection of
Dead Birds near ye Exchange, one shilling'.   But
for other men less easily pleased by rural and
domestic occupations there would have been as
much reading and as much music and as much
acting as was good for them.   Garrick was at Drury
Lane, Colman managed Covent Garden.   Johnson
and Goldsmith were busy.   Reynolds and Gainsborough were busy.   Bach and Gluck were busy.

But it is the quiet country life reflected by this
old account-book that to me is most appealing;
the suggestion of leisure that is never absent; the,
in short, simplicity of it all. 'Shoemaker for
making Shoes for my Sons and Daughters from
ye 7th of April 1765 to ye 7th of March 1766
£2-16-0', 'Jane, a Gingham Gown with gold Sprigs,
£3-15-0', 'Sylver chas'd Breeches Buckle, four and
sixpence', 'A White Silk Purse, three and sixpence', 'Kew Bridge and turnpike going in my
Post Chaise to Town and returning, two and four-
pence', 'Mrs. Chudleigh's Woman Servant, bringing a present of some Catchup, two shillings',
'Moulsey Bridge airing in my Chaise, one shilling',
and 'One year's Rate for the Watchmen and Beadles,
one pound'.

Those were the days.

ENGLAND IN 1810-11

MANY books have been written by intelligent foreigners about England, just as many Englishmen and Englishwomen have written intelligent books about other nations; but I have rarely met with a more watchful 'chiel' and social critic than Monsieur Louis Simond, who was in the United Kingdom in 1810 and 1811 and wrote an account of his travels and experiences in two large volumes, one edition in his own tongue for France, and one for England in ours. As an indication of the catholic interests of M. Simond, whose business was, I believe, shipping, I may say that he describes picture galleries and prize fights; freaks of nature (he met near Cambridge a youth measuring seven feet nine inches) and the poet Southey; country mansions and Newgate prison; Mary of Buttermere and Sydney Smith; Mr. Whitbread speaking in the House ('a stout man, brisk, rather rough, with more force than taste') and Liston and Munden acting in farce. In short, all was fish that came to his net, while the illustrations, which range from the plan of his furnished house in London and a drawing of the Needles to etchings of Welsh and Scottish peasants, are from his own hand, his conception of a Highlander being, by prevision, John Stuart Blackie to the life.

Monsieur Simond, whose interest in England may have partly been due to the circumstance that he had married an Englishwoman, landed at Falmouth early in 1810, travelling to London (which he felicitously describes as a giant so huge that a stranger can know little more than his feet) by way of Bodmin, Plymouth, Ivybridge, Exeter, Taunton, Bristol, Bath and so forth. The rate of speed, in a post-chaise, was six miles an hour—'the postboys riding instead of sitting.' He found the roads good. At Bath:

'the chaise drew up in style at the White Hart. Two well-dressed footmen were ready to help us to alight, presenting an arm on each side. Then a loud bell on the stairs, and lights carried before us to an elegantly furnished sitting-room where the fire was already blazing. In a few minutes, a neat-looking chambermaid, with an ample white apron, pinned behind, came to offer her services to the ladies and shew the bed-rooms. In less than half an hour, five powdered *gentlemen* burst into the room with three dishes, &c., and two remained to wait. I give this as a sample of the best, or rather of the finest, inns. Our bill was £2 11s. sterling, dinner for three, tea, beds and breakfast. The servants have no wages, but, depending on the generosity of travellers, they find it their interest to please them. They (the servants) cost us about five shillings a-day '.

Bath he found very beautiful: 'a great monastery, inhabited by single people, particularly super-annuated females. No trade, no manufactories, no occupations of any sort, except that of killing time, the most laborious of all. Half of the inhabitants do nothing, the other half supply them with nothings'.

In London, where he arrived in January, M. Simond was surprised by the absence of rich people, who, it seemed, were in the country, hunting, all through the dull, cold months, and did not come to town until just when the beautiful spring was making the country attractive. There were, however, enough fashionable non-hunting people left to enable him to study their customs. Here is an excellent descriptive passage of no little value to a social historian:

'In the morning all is calm,—not a mouse stirring before ten o'clock; the shops then begin to open. Milk-women, with their pails perfectly neat, suspended at the two extremities of a yoke carefully shaped to fit the shoulders, and surrounded with small tin measures of cream, ring at every door, with reiterated pulls, to hasten the maid-servants, who come half asleep to receive a measure as big as an egg, being the allowance of a family; for it is necessary to explain that milk is not here either food or drink, but a tincture, an elixir exhibited in drops, five or six at most, in a cup of tea, morning and evening. It would be difficult to say what taste or what quality these drops may impart; but so it is; and nobody thinks of questioning the propriety of the custom.

5

'Not a single carriage,—not a cart—is seen passing. The first considerable stir is the drum and military music of the Guards, marching from their barracks to Hyde Park, having at their head three or four negro giants, striking high, gracefully, and strong, the resounding cymbal. About three or four o'clock the fashionable world gives some signs of life; issuing forth to pay visits, or rather leave cards at the doors of friends never seen but in the crowd of assemblies; to go to shops, see sights, or lounge in Bond Street,—an ugly inconvenient street the attractions of which it is difficult to understand.

'At five or six they return home to dress for dinner. The streets are then lighted from one end to the other, or rather edged on either side with two long lines of little brightish dots, indicative of light, but yielding in fact very little; these are the lamps. They are not suspended in the middle of the streets as at Paris, but fixed on irons eight or nine feet high, ranged along the houses. The want of reflectors is probably the cause of their giving so little light.'

There is nothing new under the sun nor under the moon, for in his rooms in Portman Square a hundred and twenty years ago M. Simond found London's night noises as difficult to bear, in days of chairs and carriages, as we do now with motorcars and hooters. Thus:

'From six to eight the *noise* of wheels increases; it is the dinner hour. A multitude of carriages, with two eyes of flame staring in the dark before each of them, shake the pavement and the very houses, following and crossing each other at full speed. Stopping suddenly, a footman jumps down, runs to the door and lifts the heavy knocker—gives a great knock—then several smaller ones in quick succession—then with all his might

—flourishing as on a drum, with an art and an air and a delicacy of touch which denote the quality, the rank, and the fortune of his master.

'For two hours, or nearly, there is a pause; at ten a *redouble-ment* comes on. This is the great crisis of dress, of noise, and of rapidity—a universal hubbub; a sort of uniform grinding and shaking, like that experienced in a great mill with fifty pair of stones; and, if I was not afraid of appearing to exaggerate, I should say that it came upon the ear like the fall of Niagara heard at two miles distance! This crisis continues undiminished till twelve or one o'clock; then less and less during the rest of the night,—till, at the approach of day, a single carriage is heard now and then at a great distance.'

M. Simond found that London was very definitely divided into two parts:

'The trade of London is carried on in the east part of the town, called, *par excellence*, the City. The west is inhabited by people of fashion or those who wish to appear such; and the line of demar-cation, north and south, runs through Soho Square. Every minute of longitude east is equal to as many degrees of gentility *minus*, or towards west, *plus*. This meridian line north and south, like that indicated by the compass, inclines west towards the north, and east towards the south, two or three points, in such a manner, as to place a certain part of Westminster on the side of fashion; the Parliament House, Downing Street, and the Treasury, are necessarily genteel. To have a right to emigrate from east to west, it is requisite to have at least £3,000 sterling a-year; should you have less, or at least spend less, you might find yourself slighted; and £6,000 a-year would be safer. Many, indeed, have a much narrower income, who were born there; but city emigrants have not the same privileges. The legitimate people of fashion affect poverty, even, to distinguish themselves from the rich intruders.

It is citizen-like to be at ease about money, and to pay readily on demand.'

As I have said, M. Simond went everywhere and he always has something pertinent to report. Here he is in the House of Commons, where he heard the debate on the ill-fated Walcheren expedition:

'The exclamation *hear! hear! hear!* so often mentioned in the reports of speeches in the newspapers, surprised me much, the effect being quite different from what I expected. A modest, genteel *hear! hear!* is first heard from one or two voices,—others join,—more and more,—*crescendo,*—till at last a wild, tumultuous, and discordant noise pervades the whole house, resembling very nearly that of a flock of frightened geese; rising and falling, ending and beginning again, as the member happens to say anything remarkable.

'Judging from the reputed taciturnity of this nation, it might be supposed that the gravity of a legislative assembly would be more particularly observable in the British Senate; instead of which, it is the merriest place that ever was. These legislators seem perpetually on the watch for a joke; and if it can be introduced in the most serious debate, it succeeds so much the better. Some of the members, Mr. Sheridan for instance, are such complete masters of the senatorial risibility, that, by a significant word or expression of countenance, they can, when they please, put their honourable colleagues in good humour. . . . English taciturnity is not proof against a sally of wit, and still less, perhaps, against a stroke of buffoonery, called here humour.'

M. Simond winds up the matter with the generalization, 'The French are trifling and decorous, the

English grave and farcical': a pronouncement which provokes thought and which I should like to examine with minuteness. This, however, is not the time; the word is with the alert M. Simond, who continues:

'This (the English) nation is probably somewhat more think-ing, grave, solid, and taciturn than their neighbours on the other side of the channel. Less, however, than is generally supposed, —for men of all countries are not extremely unlike. In the choice of their amusements, people choose naturally something very dif-ferent from their habitual state, the tedium of which they intend to relieve; and this explains the English taste for buffoonery and broad humour.'

At one of his visits to the House M. Simond endured an all-night sitting, adjourning at half-past two a.m. to the kitchen.

'Three successive beef-steaks were broiled under our eyes, over a clear strong fire, incessantly turned, and served hot, tender, delicate, and juicy. This is a national dish, rarely good; but under this national roof it proved excellent.'

With the steaks they drank port. I am sorry that the meal was hot. How much more valuable would have been a first-hand analysis of one of Bellamy's meat pies, such as Pitt longed for on his death-bed!

Apropos the national meat, elsewhere M. Simond has a passage on John Bull as the symbolic British figure.

'This nickname, which the English have adopted for themselves, seems allusive of a certain ponderousness of body and mind, plainness and stubbornness of character, and courage deemed national; but really that portion of the people I saw lately flying before the charge of a few horse guards, looked more like a flock of sheep, than that fierce animal.'

M. Simond was attracted by English pugilism. He saw some boxing at the Fives Court between Cribb the younger, Gully and Belcher; he also visited Jackson's School. Jackson, he says, 'is the finest figure of a man I ever saw. I could not clasp with my two hands the upper part of his arm, when the biceps were swollen by the contraction of the limb.' John, or 'Gentleman', Jackson, who numbered Byron among his pupils, had been champion of England from 1795 to 1803; he was now, in 1810, forty-one. His height was five feet eleven inches, and he weighed fourteen stone. As an instance of his strength it is recorded that with an eighty-four-pound weight depending from the little finger of his right hand, he could sign his name with steadiness and clarity.

Later M. Simond saw a real prize fight. It was at Moulsey Hurst and the combatants were Tom Molineaux the negro and Rimmer of Lancashire. A huge ring of wagons and other vehicles had been formed, and, having bargained for places on a cart, the Frenchman and his companions mounted it and had a good view. Rimmer made his appearance quietly, but Molineaux arrived on the box of a barouche and four, muffled in great coats and accompanied by young men of fashion.

'Here began a scene quite unexpected to me, the clearing of the ring. All the boxers in town, professional and amateurs, charged the mob at once, which, giving way in confusion, formed a sort of irregular circle outside the rope-ring, but not large enough. With sticks and whips applied *sans cérémonie* these champions of the fist pressed back the compact mass. I expected every moment a general engagement; nothing of the kind, the mob shrunk from the flogging, but without resentment. 'Tis true, the blows appeared to be directed mostly over the heads of the first ranks and fell on those five or six deep; the weapons being mostly coachmen's or carters' long whips. These rear-ranks, assailed by an invisible hand, had no resource but a retreat, and made way for those in front; the latter, squatting down on the turf, formed, at last, a sort of barrier over which the crowd could see.'

The progress of the fight, well described, I find too sanguinary to transcribe. Half-way through, it was interrupted for at least twenty minutes by the invasion of the mob, who carried stage, ropes and everything before them. Order, however, being resumed, the battle proceeded until Molineaux knocked his opponent out. 'Hats flew, cries rent the air; the black, meantime, grinning over his fallen adversary in Homeric triumph.'

It is a pity that the Frenchman's very wide interests did not extend to cricket, for, had they done so, we might have an eye-witness's account of one of the matches at Lord's in 1810: that on May 29, 30 and 31, for instance, between Lord Frederick Beauclerk's side and the Hon. E. Bligh's, when William Lambert made 132 not out and William Beldham ('Silver Billy') 52. Or the single-wicket match on July 6 and 7 between Mr. Osbaldeston ('The Squire') and Lambert as partners against Lord Frederick Beauclerk and T. C. Howard. It would be valuable to have a description of what then happened, for the match was made historic first by Mr. Osbaldeston's illness, which rendered him unable to play; next by Lord Frederick Beauclerk's refusal to postpone; next by his refusal to allow a substitute to field; and finally by Lambert's personal triumph, for he won by 15 runs and took the whole stakes, £100. 'Lambert', says *Scores and Biographies*, 'bowled wides purposely to Lord F. Beauclerk "in order to put him out of temper", in which he succeeded, and thus aided the match being won.' Wides at that time—and indeed till 1827—were excluded from the score.

But I am wandering far from M. Simond, who on the evening of the day on which he had seen Molineaux knock out Rimmer went to Covent Garden to hear Catalani. His description of the licence then permitted in one section of that theatre reads oddly to-day, when there is no longer such a thing as a promenade lounge in any London music-hall. Here is his account of the gallery:

'That part of the upper region which fronts the stage is occupied by a less indecent, but more noisy, sort of people; sailors, footmen, low tradesmen and their wives and mistresses, who enjoy themselves, drinking, whistling, howling as much as they please. These gods, for so they are called from their elevated station, which is in France denominated the *paradis*, assume the high prerogative of hurling down their thunder on both actors and spectators, in the shape of nut-shells, cores of apples, and orange-peel. This innocent amusement has always been considered in England as a sort of exuberance of liberty, of which it is well to have a little too much, to be sure that you have enough. Some persons complain even that the gods are become much too tame and tractable and like the French tenants of the *paradis*,—a good thing in itself, but a bad omen.'

On another evening M. Simond saw *Hamlet* played by John Philip Kemble, with two other of the comic actors whom Lamb has analysed and extolled for us—Munden and Fawcett. His account of the performance, with its defence of the English affection for comedy mixed with tragedy, is illuminating and sagacious:

'Hamlet was acted yesterday at Covent Garden, and Kemble, the reigning prince of the English stage, filled the principal part. He understands his art thoroughly, but wants spirit and nature. His manner is precise and artificial; his voice monotonous and wooden; his features are too large, even for the stage.

'Munden in the part of Polonius, and Fawcett in the grave-digger played charmingly. It is enough to mention the grave-diggers, to awaken in France the cry of rude and barbarous taste; and, were I to say how the part is acted, it might be still worse. After beginning their labour, and breaking ground for a grave, a conversation begins between the two grave-diggers. The chief one takes off his coat, folds it carefully, and puts it by in a safe corner; then, taking up his pick-axe, spits in his hand,—gives a stroke or two,—talks,—stops,—strips off his waistcoat, still talking, —folds it with great deliberation and nicety, and puts it with the coat,—then an under-waistcoat, still talking,—another and another. I counted seven or eight, each folded and unfolded very leisurely, in a manner always different, and with gestures faithfully copied from nature. The British public enjoys this scene excessively, and the pantomimic variations a good actor knows how to intro-duce in it are sure to be vehemently applauded.

'The French admit of no such relaxation in the *dignité tragique*:

"L'étroite bienséance y veut être gardée";

and Boileau did not even allow Molière to have won the prize of comedy, because he had

"Quitté pour le bouffon l'agréable et le fin
Et sans honte à Terence allié Tabarin",

much less would he or his school have approved of an alliance between tragedy and farce. Yet it may well be questioned whether the interest is best kept up by an uninterrupted display of eleva-tion. For my part, I am inclined to think that the repose afforded by a comic episode renovates the powers of attention and of feel-ing, and prepares for new tragical emotions more effectually than an attempt to protract these emotions during the whole represen-tation could have done.'

Among the curiosities of the English stage must always be ranked Master Betty, the son of a well-to-do inhabitant of Shrewsbury, who became the chief of the world's infantine phenomena. At the age of ten, in 1801, seeing Mrs. Siddons in one of her most moving parts, he vowed that he would die if he were not allowed to act too, and so determined was he that in 1803 he was on the stage. That was in Belfast, in Voltaire's *Zara.* His début was a riot, and he continued to enchant the Irish, and even the hard-headed Scotch in Glasgow and Edinburgh, James Home, the author of *Douglas,* in which the boy played Norval, declaring that he had never seen the character properly handled before. Master Betty reached London in 1804, when he was thirteen, and, again as Norval, carried the town off its feet, bringing record sums to the exchequer of Drury Lane, and being received at Court. The House of Commons was on one occasion adjourned to give the members the opportunity of seeing him as Hamlet.

By 1810, when M. Simond saw him, a fellow-visitor to a picture gallery, Master Betty was twenty and his vogue was over. He was, in short, Mr. Betty.

'He is a great calf; ill made, knock-kneed, a pretty face, fresh, round, and rosy, without expression, or any perceivable trace of sentiment or genius. I suspect there must have been much exaggeration in the fashionable enthusiasm displayed on the occasion, as well as a great fund of bad taste. The cleverest child that ever was can at best mimic passions which he never felt; and at the height of your fallacious raptures, merely his face and figure afford you irrefragable proofs that you are the dupe of a shallow counterfeit and perfect *mystification* of sentiment.'

After some indifferent success on the stage as a grown man, Betty left it altogether when he was thirty-four. Thereafter he lived quietly and happily, enjoying his fortune and often laughing at his early adulation, until 1874, when he died.

I mentioned Lamb just now, and, if I am peculiarly interested in M. Simond's account of the Persian Ambassador, it is for an Elian connotation:

'We have here a Persian ambassador, who furnishes a good deal of conversation to the fashionable world; the ladies love his fine black beard, his broken English, and odd good humour. His *propos* are much repeated. He complains that there are none but old women in England; the young ones not being so much in company. He likes *embonpoint*, and exclaims: "Ah! nice fat, nice fat!" Of a pretty woman he said, "She is a nice little fellow." A young lady was sent to sit by him on a sofa, and talk to him; the conversation being exhausted, and he perceiving she was tired, or being so himself, said, "Now, my dear, it is well; you may go." . . . During the Walcheren business, he took it for granted that the heads of the ministers would be off.'

This interests me because it is the same Persian ambassador about whom Lamb used to be funny. Writing to Manning on 2nd January, 1810, he said:

'The Persian ambassador is the principal thing talked of now. I sent some people to see him worship the sun on Primrose Hill at half-past six in the morning, 28th November; but he did not come, which makes me think the old fire-worshippers are a sect almost extinct in Persia. Have you trampled on the Cross yet? The Persian ambassador's name is Shaw Ali Mirza. The common people call him Shaw Nonsense.' Among the people upon whom Lamb played his practical joke was poor George Dyer.

The scientific pundits of the Royal Institution drew M. Simond's attention no less than the Molesey Hurst bruisers, and he is interesting about its presiding genius, Mr. Davy, afterwards Sir Humphry. The Royal Institution had been founded in Albemarle Street by Count Rumford in 1799, and in 1801 Davy was engaged as a residential lecturer. He was then twenty-three, fresh from Cornwall, with the Cornish burr still on his lips, and full of enthusiasm and energy and inspiration. Gradually he won his way, not only as an experimentalist and inventor, but as an orator. People thronged to hear him speak, almost as they had thronged to see Master Betty.

'Mr. Davy's lectures at the Royal Institution are still more crowded than they were last year, and the lecturer himself more than ever sought after by the great and the fair. It would be a matter of great regret if the allurements of science should at last prove inferior to those of fashion, and if future fame should be sacrificed to ephemeral successes. The elocution of this celebrated chemist is very different from the usual tone of men of science in England; his lectures are frequently figurative and poetical; and he is occasionally carried away by the natural tendency of his subject, and of his genius, into the depths of moral philosophy and of religion. . . . The voice and manner of Mr. Davy are rather gentle, than impressive and strong; he knows what nature has given him, and what it has withheld, and husbands his means accordingly. You may always foresee by a certain tuning or pitching of the organ of speech to a graver key, thrusting his chin into his neck, and even pulling out his cravat, when Mr. Davy is going to be eloquent—for he rarely yields to the inspiration till he is duly prepared.'

Thinking it 'incumbent upon him' to see something of the prisons of London, M. Simond went to Newgate.

'A turnkey took me up a back stair-case to the leads, from which, like Asmodeus in the *Diable Boiteux*, I had a view into the interior, and could see what was doing in the different divisions of this melancholy abode. We first perched upon the debtors' ward; they sat and walked about in two courts, paved with flag-stones, and very clean; the women separated from the men. Some of the women (they were few) held up their hands for alms. . . . Then we went to the felons under sentence of death. They were playing fives against the wall of a narrow court; their irons fastened on one leg only, from the knee to the ankle, over a sort of cushion, and so arranged as to make no noise, and to be no impediment at all to their motions; in fact a mere matter of form,—and so is also, in a great degree, the sentence of death itself. Not one of these people appeared to believe it serious. One of them, whose companions were lately executed for forgery, had been reprieved the day before, having turned evidence, and they were all playing with great briskness and glee. . . . The transportation ladies, crowded in a small court, were much more disorderly than the men. They threatened and wrangled among themselves, singing, vociferating, and, as much as the narrow space allowed, moving about in all sorts of dresses,—one of them in men's clothes. They are not in irons like the men. In a more spacious court, separated from these women by a high wall, were state prisoners, as my guide called them, playing fives (the favourite pastime of Newgate it seems).'

I have mentioned elsewhere, in an essay on the name of Hatfield, how M. Simond saw at Newgate the would-be regicide, James Hatfield, who had fired at George III in Drury Lane Theatre in 1800. In 1810 he was foreman of his prison ward at a salary of a guinea a week: 'happy as a king,' said the turnkey. Another prisoner, whose state hardly called for much pity, was the editor and proprietor of a paper which M. Simond was in the habit of reading—*The Weekly Register*—who had recently been fined £1,000 and sentenced to two years' imprisonment for an article on flogging in the Army.

'I inquired for Mr. Cobbett, expecting to see him among the gentlemen.—*Oh! no,* said my turnkey, *he is too great for that. Where is he then? Why he is in the governor's house,—I'll show you,—plenty of money, and that is everything, you know.* Then walking farther on the leads, he showed me a grated door, through which I could see a carpeted room, Mr. Cobbett's room. He has the key of the grated door, and therefore free access to this leaden roof, which is extensive, high, and airy, with a most beautiful view of St. Paul's, and over great part of the city. His family is with him, and he continues to pour out his torrent of abuse as freely as ever, on every thing and every body in turn.'

Cobbett, as a matter of fact, had offered to discontinue his paper and thus evade punishment; but the Government or the Law Courts wouldn't have it. Could a more comic situation be imagined?

Said M. Simond:

'The freedom of the press is considered in England as the palladium of national liberty; on the other hand, the abuse of it is undoubtedly its curse. It is the only plague, somebody has said, which Moses forgot to inflict upon Egypt.'

—that was a little over a hundred and twenty years ago.

Although London was M. Simond's headquarters, he made several journeys into the country and even reached Scotland and Ireland, taking some useful introductions.

'We had the pleasure of seeing several times the celebrated Mr. Southey, a distinguished favourite of the English muses. Mr. Coleridge, whose talents are equally known, although less fruitful, was at Mr. S.'s, with whom he has some family connection. Both of these gentlemen, and, I believe, Mr. Wordsworth, another of the poets of the lakes, had, in the warmth of their youthful days, some fifteen years ago, taken the spirited resolution of traversing the Atlantic, in order to breathe the pure air of liberty in the

United States. Some accident delayed the execution of this laudable project, and gave them time to cool. At present, these gentlemen seem to think that there is no need of going so far for liberty, and that there is a reasonable allowance of it at home. Their democracy is come down to Whiggism, and may not even stop there.'

It is a calamity that Mr. Coleridge is merely mentioned: but M. Simond was not a romantic. He had far more opinions than feelings and preferred facts to fancy, so that rather than talk with the author of *The Ancient Mariner* he discussed with Mr. Southey the legend of the *Cid* and was pleased to be instructed as to a misunderstanding he had long cherished. Mention of the Frenchman occurs in a letter of Southey's in 1816, in which he comments on Monsieur S.'s 'liveliness and perverse good sense' and observes at the same time that he said that Milton's and Southey's poems had few readers, although many admirers.

It is odd and lamentable that Wordsworth does not appear on the scene at all. In Edinburgh, however, one of his friends is described: the author of the '*Waverley* novels':

'We could not be at Edinburgh without wishing to see the Caledonian bard whose fertile and brilliant genius produces poems with the rapidity of thought,—and we have been gratified. Mr. Scott is a tall and stout man, thirty-five or forty years of age; very lame from some accident in his early youth. His countenance is not particularly poetical,—complexion fair, with a coarse skin,—

6

little beard,—sandy hair,—and light eyes and eye-brows;—the
tout ensemble rather dull and heavy. Yet when he speaks, which
he is not always disposed to do, and is animated, his eye lightens up

"With all a poet's ecstasy."

This poet likes conviviality, and tells well, and *con amore*, such
stories as are told here only after dinner. He is a great tory.'

On the way back from Scotland M. Simond
met a remarkable man, whose identity he thinks
to conceal under the initials S. S. This was, of
course, Sydney Smith.

'We had the pleasure of seeing here a preacher of another sort,
the Rev. S. S., who has been the delight of the devout fashionables
of the capital. It is not, however, in this character we have known
him, but in his own house, where, among his friends, he is a most
agreeable companion. He has the reputation of being one of the
most lively writers of the *Edinburgh Review*, and serious too when
he pleases. His countenance struck me as very like that of the
unfortunate Louis XVI, with more vivacity in the eye.'

The next day Sydney Smith took M. Simond to
the Quaker Asylum at York, the Retreat, where
he made the statement that 'there was an undue
proportion of tailors among mad people'. M.
Simond seems to have been uncertain how to
receive this information; and, indeed, he was in
dangerous company. 'I would not answer', he
says, 'that this remark was to be taken seriously.
The profession has a certain degree of ridicule
attached to it in England, and is obnoxious to

certain jokes, which, although neither very new nor
very refined, genuine mirth is not so fastidious as
to disdain.'

I should say that my attention was drawn to
Simond's book by a scathing reference to it in
one of Miss Ferrier's letters, describing it as 'a
compilation of old newspapers, Travellers' Guides,
Joe Miller jests, impertinent gossip and vulgar
scurrility, all tacked together in the most grating
disjointed style that sets our teeth on edge and
makes them feel as if they were trotting on the
back of a donkey'. The reader must, I think,
agree with me that there is much injustice here.
Simond, whom Miss Ferrier calls Simeon, is better
than that; in fact, his book is singularly free from
any of those defects. She attacks him for describing Glencoe as 'having fine steps with a green
carpet spread upon them; that it is well swept and
free from litter'. Simond's words are:

'It is a deep solitary valley, without trees, without cultivation,
but of the most lively verdure, which creeps up the steep sides of
the mountains on each side, interrupted by steps or terraces of
black rocks, more and more frequent as the eye ascends; the green
carpet spreads over each of them, till the whole is blended in the
distance, or rather elevation; and the highest summits are termin-
ated by black caps of broken rocks, frequently enveloped in heavy
clouds. The haziness of the atmosphere spread a singular soft-
ness and faintness over the whole scene. No crumbling stones,
or poor fragments, littered the even surface. The lawn is swept

clean and rolled, but it is by the hand of Nature, which is never trim and formal.'

'The nightingale', Miss Ferrier continues her charge, 'he says sings in a vulgar manner.' But he qualifies the word. Here is the passage:

'We have heard here (Hertford) the nightingale for the first time in England. Fancy had embellished the faded recollection in my mind. I imagined it a long uninterrupted tale of woe, the note deep and strong, but soft, tender, and melancholy; instead of which, it is a quick succession of strong, sharp, brisk notes. Shrill whistling occurs very often, not unlike the blackbird. There is indeed a sort of water-note, which is very beautiful, approaching what I had imagined, but it is so soon interrupted by another quite different, that you have not time to enjoy it. Upon the whole it is a lively, pleasing, vulgar sort of melody, inferior perhaps to the singing of other birds of less fame. The circumstances of night and silence, and the trite allusions of the poets, have contributed to this adventitious fame of Philomel. Contrary to what I should have supposed, the nightingale is heard to more advantage near than far off.'

—That is not too bad, but for the author of *Marriage* my Frenchman could do nothing right. Alas, poor Simeon, who, as it happens, should he have had cause to mention Miss Ferrier, would have spelt her rightly, for he is not of the Gallic tradition with regard to English proper names. All the same I should like to see the copy of his work to which she alludes 'enriched with her marginal notes'.

Let me end my quotations from this entertaining

observer with a passage on books, which, were it rather better expressed, as it probably is in the French version, would take its place in any compilation devoted to the praises of reading:

'Whatever they may say, nobody talks so well or so agreeably as a book, and they would allow it themselves, in regard to their own book. Where can you find so easy and discreet a friend and companion? You may interrupt the conversation when you please, —take a nap,—renew it again where you left it,—go back to what interests you,—skip what does not,—and shut yourself up with that friend, sure of never having more of him than you like. This consciousness of safety is inestimable. To judge of it, consider only with what avidity the printed letters of eminent persons are read, and reflect on the dread and consternation the sight of these same letters in the original manuscript would have produced;— just drawn from the pocket of the person to whom they were written, and about to be read to you in confidence!'

M. Simond, I might add, died at Geneva in 1831.

THE ENGLISH GAME

'The boys are marking out the crease,
So fumble for your lucky piece
    And send her upward spinning.
O give me Spring for life and love,
A skylark singing up above,
    And cricket just beginning.'

                                G. D. MARTINEAU

WHEN Merrie England held tournaments and archery competitions, and broke each other's knuckles and heads with single-sticks, there was no cricket; but there were games with the rudiments of cricket in them, not unrelated to Bat and Trap, from which it gradually evolved. Let historians be consulted; my concern here is not with remote and dark origins or the crude stages of development, but with the game after its infancy was done: cricket in its lusty youth, cricket in its fixed glamorous maturity as we know it now.

I have read that the actual word 'cricket' or 'crickett' is first found in the middle of the sixteenth century, and a hundred years later two such different characters as Bishop Ken and Gargantua were both

76

playing the game: the Bishop as a schoolboy at Winchester, and Rabelais' hero in France. But if I am a little doubtful of the Frenchman's ability, it is not so much because I have watched some of the games played every Sunday in summer in the environs of Paris, as because Urquhart, Rabelais' translator, in his desire to make his English version as natural and national as possible, used words very freely.

Cricket, for our purposes, began with the eighteenth century. The earliest first-class cricket club that we know of was founded in 1700 at the Artillery Fields at Finsbury; the first score to be preserved is that of a match between Kent and All England on the Finsbury ground on 18th June, 1744, when Kent won by one wicket. The captain of Kent was Lord John Frederick Sackville of Knole, afterwards third Duke of Dorset, who very soon after this match was to busy himself with the Hambledon Cricket Club, in Hampshire, which is usually called the Cradle of the Game, although the mere fact that the 1744 match was played against a whole eleven from Kent shows that the babe had already been weaned elsewhere.

Looking at the All England side we find two Harrises whom we may assume to be Hampshire men, probably antecedents of the famous David Harris of the Hambledon Club who flourished in

the 1780's, and two others—Newlands—one of
whom, R. Newland, was almost certainly the
Richard Newland of Slindon, in Sussex, who taught
Richard Nyren how to play; and Richard Nyren,
under the Duke of Dorset, was the mainstay of
the Hambledon Club when in 1750 it began to be
a power. But of him I say more in the essay on
John Nyren which follows this. The year 1744
was important also as being that in which the first
laws of the game were drawn up, although they
were not issued officially by the M.C.C. until 1787.

London, despite activity elsewhere, chiefly in
Kent, Sussex and Hampshire, became the official
head-quarters of the game, the Finsbury ground
giving place to White Conduit Fields about 1780,
and seven years later to a ground on what is now
Dorset Square, which had been laid out by a player
and attendant at White Conduit Fields, named
Thomas Lord, a Scotchman, who, when we are
casting about for the great influences of cricket,
must always be mentioned.

In 1814 Thomas Lord carried his turf to St.
John's Wood, to the new ground of the Marylebone
Cricket Club, or the M.C.C., which now bears his
name—Lord's. And the M.C.C. has been the
lawgiver of cricket ever since.

What we should know of cricket in the second
half of the eighteenth century would be meagre and

anaemic indeed but for the fortunate circumstance that Richard Nyren, who was a Hampshire farmer, had a very intelligent and observant son named John. This lad at an early age was allowed to join the Hambledon Club as what he calls a 'farmer's pony'; he remained in it and of it until it broke up in 1791, and in old age he communicated his recollections to a practised writer. His book, *The Young Cricketer's Tutor*, published in 1833, enables us vividly to reconstruct the Hambledon Eleven and to share in the simple enthusiastic spirit of those times.

Cricket as then played, when the grass was cut with a scythe and not rolled, and the bowlers who won the toss pitched the wickets according to the mole-hills and hollows that might favour them, and the batsmen with their curved implements went for everything, led to far more festive occasions than those to which we are accustomed, where the conditions are so precise. The desire to win was not less keen than now—probably keener—but there was a gayer hit-or-miss spirit. For the early batsmen—the great cricketers of John Nyren's boyhood —had but one stroke, and that was what we call to-day a slog or swipe. Along came the ball, delivered underhand over the uneven turf, and they lashed at it. In fact, except that contact with the ground intervened between bowler and hitter, early cricket must have been very like American baseball at the present moment, where everything is in the hitting, and defensive play is merely tactical and sacrificial, in the interests of the men at base.

Richard Nyren's sagacity and all-round ability were no doubt invaluable, but in actual proficiency he was surpassed, with the ball, by David Harris and Edward Stevens (known as 'Lumpy'), and with the bat by several of his side, of whom I may single out only William Beldham, nicknamed 'Silver Billy', and John Small, a gamekeeper from Petersfield. These were the four greatest Hambledon players.

John Small must be added to the pioneers I have already mentioned, by reason of an innovating ingenuity which entitles him to be called roundly the Father of Modern Cricket; for, according to Beldham, talking in old age (and he lived to be well over ninety), it was Small who first changed from a curved bat to a straight, and he did this partly to introduce defensive play, until then unknown, and partly to add to his repertory a stroke that was also a novelty, the draw, which held its place for many years but is now no longer seen. It consisted in deflecting the ball between the wicket and the legs. I remember Charlwood of Sussex being very apt at it in the eighteen-seventies —but it has now passed in favour of the glide, which was brought to perfection by Ranjitsinhji.

John Small was born in 1737, and thus was

thirteen when the Hambledon Club was founded, making his first appearance in 1755. In 1774, for Hambledon against Kent, he made 18 and 55 not out, while in 1776 he was at the head of the averages with 416 for 12 innings. The first recorded match in which he played was for Hambledon against Caterham, when he made 80; the last for Hambledon was in 1793, against the M.C.C., when he made only 2 and 0; but he played in London now and then after that. He was expert in other ways besides cricket: he was a fine skater and a true shot, and Nyren tells us of his skill as a musician both with the voice and the violin. Indeed, he once became a very Orpheus and by his melody subdued an angry bull. Beginning as a shoemaker, he became a gamekeeper and latterly took to making bats and balls. The last six balls from his manufactory were bought by Mr. E. H. Budd, of the M.C.C., to whom Mr. William Ward, also of the M.C.C., offered a guinea apiece for them. When Small died, on 31st December, 1826, a poet wrote an epitaph beginning:

'Here lies, bowled out by Death's unerring ball,
A cricketer renowned, by name John Small.'

To retrace our steps, let me say that at first the bat might be of any size, but a Mr. White of Reigate, having turned up at a match with a blade exactly as wide as the wicket, it was decided to make a fixed limit of 4½ inches. At first the stumps numbered only two, one of which the ball had to hit; but after a match which John Small had won off his own bat, in 1775, they were increased to three—the reason being that the ball passed innocuously between them so often that the losing side, brooding over the anomaly, came to the conclusion that some injustice was afoot and that it should be remedied. Small, although less consciously, was thus, on this occasion, again a pioneer.

All the bowling in these early days of the game was underhand, fast or slow, guileful or direct. An effort, made somewhere about 1790, by Tom Walker, one of the Hambledon Club, to raise his arm, met with such antagonism that he lowered it again; but in 1806 Mr. John Willes, of Sutton Valence in Kent, introduced round-arm bowling, although at head-quarters it was not tolerated in any form until after 1827, and not fully until 1844. The present style of bowling, in which the arm may be raised as high as one likes so long as the elbow is not bent, came in in 1864 and has never changed since. One sees no more of the old round-arm, but underhand bowling is still met with now and then. Indeed, there have been until quite recent days very destructive lob-bowlers, notably Walter Humphreys of Sussex, G. H. Simpson-Hayward

FULLER PILCH
After a Drawing made by George Frederick Watts for 'Felix', in the Pavilion at Lord's

of Worcestershire, and D. L. A. Jephson of Surrey.

There had, as usual, to be martyrs before full liberty was won. John Willes, the inventor of round-arm bowling, although he was bowling it without interference in country matches and had shown the way to William Lambert and James Broadbridge and to William Lillywhite, the greatest of its exponents, known as the 'Nonpareil', was no-balled when he appeared at Lord's in 1823, and was so angry that he leapt on his horse, left the ground and never played again. Cricketers can still be angry, but horses, alas! no longer are leapt on. Instead there are letters to the papers and even representations to the M.C.C.

Not until some trial games had been played in 1827 was underhand superseded at Lord's. Again, in 1862, it was the no-balling of Edgar Willsher of Kent, for lifting his hand too high, that led, two years later, to the new law. The game was over for that day, but on the next was resumed, not with a new bowler but a new umpire!

I have said that it was John Small of Hambledon who was the inventor of the straight bat. Another of his Hambledon colleagues, William Fennex, claimed to be the first batsman to step out to a ball and deal with it before it had time to rise: to the horror of his father, a traditionalist. 'Hey,

hey, boy!' he cried, 'what's this? Do you call that play?' And it was a pupil of Fennex, after he had gone to live in Suffolk—the youthful Fuller Pilch (1803–70)—who was destined to develop the art of batting still further. Cricketers are adaptable and forceful men, always trying experiments, and we may be sure that with the straight bat as an ally they soon added many strokes. But it was not until Fuller Pilch that forward play became general. In the records of batting his name stands perhaps highest until we come to that of W. G. Grace.

Pilch, who, although associated chiefly with Kent, was known all over the country by reason of his single-wicket contests against this and that champion, was not only a model of elegance and accomplishment, but he was a man of sterling character, such as all cricketers, in the days when matches were played for money, did not show themselves to be. In fact, William Lambert of Surrey, one of the best all-round performers in the first years of the nineteenth century, was banned from Lord's on account of a charge of corruption. There is no financial incitement at work to-day, and let us be glad of it; but I always regret the loss of the single-wicket contests which were such a feature of the game in the first half of the last century. With our very full programme of inter-county matches there is normally no time for these trials of strength and skill between the all-rounders; but whenever a match ends on the second day, or early on the third, challenges surely might be given and the issue tried.

Having no record of any other of the pioneer clubs to correspond with Nyren's, we have to rely on *Lillywhite's Scores and Biographies* (whose early pages are full of single-wicket games) for information concerning the greatest players at the beginning of the last century, when the bat was at last straight, and balls were blocked, and slogging had given way to thoughtful attack, and round-arm bowling had come in to make the batsman's task harder.

The greatest names between 1800 and the rise of Fuller Pilch are those of Mr. William Ward, of the M.C.C., a wealthy amateur who made Lord's ground safe for posterity; 'Squire' Osbaldeston, of the M.C.C.; the Rev. Lord Frederick Beauclerk, of the M.C.C.; the Hon. E. Bligh, of Kent; Mr. B. Aislabie, of the M.C.C.; John Bowyer, of Surrey; Mr. Herbert Jenner, afterwards Jenner-Fust, of the M.C.C.; Mr. C. J. Harenc, of Kent; William Beldham, William Fennex, Tom Walker, T. C. Howard, of Hants; T. Beagley, of Hants; James Broadbridge, of Sussex; Mr. E. H. Budd, of the M.C.C.; and William Lambert, perhaps the finest all-round performer of them all, to whom I have alluded not only in this essay but in that on 'England in 1810–11'. We have seen something of the interdependence of cricket in the cases of Richard Nyren learning from Richard Newland and Fuller Pilch from Fennex; 'from Lambert', said William Clarke, who, with William Lillywhite, was the deadliest slow bowler (one under-arm and one round-arm) of the first half of the nineteenth century, 'I learnt more than from any man alive'. Thus the good work goes on.

Frederick William Lillywhite deserves very special mention for the fight he made for round-arm bowling and for the integrity of his cricketing career. Born in 1792, near Goodwood in Sussex, he played his first match at Lord's in 1827, coming to head-quarters later than any other cricketer of renown. Before this he had been the mainstay of various Sussex elevens, and it was he more than any other performer who brought about the change in the Laws in 1828. After doing much to develop cricket at Brighton, he moved to London in 1844 and thereafter was intimately associated with the M.C.C. 'Me bowling' (pronounced to rhyme with howling), 'Pilch batting and Box keeping wicket —that', he said, 'is cricket.' Among the many thousands of balls bowled by the 'Nonpareil' there were only 6 wides. It was he who remarked that if he always bowled his best—or 'thought every ball'—no one would ever get a run. When he

ALFRED MYNN

From an Engraving by C. Hunt

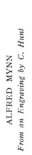

WILLIAM LILLYWHITE,
'THE NONPAREIL', AT LORD'S IN 1853

From an Engraving in the Pavilion

died, in 1854, the M.C.C. erected a tomb to him in Highgate Cemetery which, for its simple nobility and the testimony of its inscription, should be an object of pilgrimage for every schoolboy.

Mention of Box reminds me of an injustice both in written memories of great deeds in cricket and in conversation about the game, and there are few better forms of talk: the tendency to lay all the emphasis on batting. We remember with more vividness, or describe with more gusto, the gallant innings and the terrific sixes than the feats of bowlers and fieldsmen. This preferential treatment of batsmen may be natural, but it is not fair. All three departments of the game are interdependent and of equal importance; but where the balance is in most need of adjustment is in the case of the wicket-keeper, whom there is a kind of tacit conspiracy to overlook or, more accurately, to take for granted. But the wicket-keeper is, of course, a corner-stone. If he fails, the side will be in the greatest danger; if he is competent, the bowlers are worth many per cent. more. The first great wicket-keeper was this Thomas Box of Sussex, who 'kept' for many years to William Lillywhite's bowling, and soon after him came E. G. Wenman of Kent. Later stumpers of immortal fame are Pooley of Surrey, Pinder of Yorkshire, Pilling of Lancashire, Phillips of Sussex, Lilley of Warwick-

7

shire, Strudwick of Surrey and Henry Martyn of
Oxford and Somerset, who could also hit as hard as
any man may who is not played for his batting.   At
the present moment there are Duckworth of Lancashire and Ames of Kent, who is a great batsman
too.   Among other great historical names are the
superb and fearless Blackham, the Australian, who
died only the other day, in 1932, the Hon. Alfred
Lyttelton, and Gregor McGregor of Cambridge and
Middlesex, who captained his side from behind
the stumps—an ideal place for the man in control.
As long ago as 1844 William Lillywhite was
writing, in his *Young Cricketers' Guide*, 'Advise
with the wicket-keeper as to the position of the
fieldsmen; he can best assist your wishes by *silently*
shifting the men unknown to the batsman.'

The greatest of Fuller Pilch's contemporaries, in
every sense of the word, was Alfred Mynn of Kent,
who, on his tombstone at Thornham, where he was
buried in 1861, is called 'the Champion of English
Cricketers'—and not without reason, for twice he
met and defeated at single-wicket the claimant of
that title, T. Marsden of Sheffield.   Mynn, who
weighed eighteen stone, bowled the fastest round-
arm ball and hit harder than any one in England.
A third Kentish player of genius was Nicholas
Wanostrocht, who called himself Felix and who
not only was an all-round proficient in the field but

wrote a classic of the game called *Felix on the Bat*.[1]
Felix had immense influence on the game by popu-
larizing cutting and inventing batting-gloves. An
amateur artist, it was he who gave us the portrait
of William Clarke that I reproduce.

Among other famous players in the days of Fuller
Pilch and Alfred Mynn and Felix were Mynn's
brother Walter, the finest long-stop of his time
(long-stop being a very necessary person when
Alfred was bowling); William Martingell of Surrey
and Kent, Felix's pupil, who in old age became a
cricket tutor at Eton; John Wisden the Sussex
bowler, who succeeded George Brown of Sussex,
said to be the fastest bowler of all time; William
Searle of Surrey, the batsman; James Cobbett of
Surrey, the all-rounder; Joseph Guy of Notts, who
had such a polished style that he might have played
'in the Queen's parlour'; Samuel Redgate of Notts,
the bowler; William Dorington of Kent, the batsman; the Hon. R. Grimston, the Harrovian; James
Grundy, the Notts all-rounder; and William Clarke,
also of Notts, the bowler and strategist.

[1] When living at Blackheath, where he kept a school, Wanostrocht, or Felix, befriended the youthful George Frederick Watts,
afterwards the R.A. and English Old Master; and Watts made to
his specification the series of drawings of batsmen in action which
appear in the book. Four depict Felix himself, Fuller Pilch and
Alfred Mynn being also represented. Five of the originals hang
in the Pavilion at Lord's.

This William Clarke, or Old Clarke, of Notting-
ham, deserves special notice, for he occupies another
of the niches in the cricket Valhalla. At a time
when round-arm was becoming general, and indeed
necessary if the bat was not to be, as we say, on
top, he continued to bowl underhand with such
cunning and accuracy that his victims were legion.
In 1850, for instance, when he was fifty-one, he
took, in thirty matches, three hundred and three
wickets. But he was more than a bowler: he wrote
very shrewdly on the game; as the landlord of the
Trent Bridge inn and owner of the ground there,
he was the father of the Nottinghamshire County
Cricket Club, and in 1846 he did the best possible
work towards increasing cricket's vogue throughout the country—and especially in the North, which
had been far behind the South in zeal—by found-
ing the All England Eleven. This team, which
included the best man in every department, began
on August 31st of that year by playing Twenty
of Sheffield, and it continued to wage warfare
against similar numerical odds for some seasons.
Internal trouble led to a rival organization, the
United All England Eleven, being formed in 1852,
its first match being in June against Twenty
Gentlemen of Hampshire; while in 1865 the United
South of England Eleven arose and began its
career with a match against Twenty-two of Ireland.

WILLIAM, OR 'OLD' CLARKE
From an Engraving after the Portrait by 'Felix'

Thus did cricket extend to the provinces and consolidate its position as the English national game.

We come now to the eighteen-fifties and sixties. William Lillywhite was still bowling, Fuller Pilch and Alfred Mynn were for a while still batting. Other great exponents of the game were Sir Frederick Bathurst of Hants, James and John Lillywhite of Sussex, T. Lockyer the Surrey wicket-keeper, Edgar Willsher the Kent bowler, George Parr of Notts, the finest leg-hitter of his own or any day—hitting to leg now having become, to the game's loss, largely superseded by the hook or the glance, which, beautiful as the stroke is, does not really atone; William Caffyn of Surrey, Julius Cæsar of Surrey, Mr. David Buchanan, the great amateur bowler, Christopher Tinley and John Jackson of Notts ('Jackson's pace is very fearful'), H. H. Stephenson of Surrey, Tom Hayward and George Tarrant of Cambridgeshire, and the Rev. C. D. Marsham of Kent and Mr. V. E. Walker (the oldest of the famous brothers of Middlesex), both very tricky bowlers.

In the next ten years we find at the top Edward Pooley the Surrey wicket-keeper, W. Mycroft of Derbyshire, George Pinder the Yorkshire wicket-keeper, Harry Jupp the Surrey batsman, Alfred Shaw the Nottinghamshire bowler, George Freeman the Yorkshire bowler, W. Oscroft of Notts, Mr. C. A. Absolom of Kent, Ephraim Lockwood of

Yorkshire, Southerton the Surrey slow bowler and Richard Daft of Notts, one of the most graceful and punishing bats ever seen.

And so we reach the greatest figure of all in the history of the game—William Gilbert Grace, who, when he was a boy of five, was encouraged and stimulated at Bristol by seeing Old Clarke take eighteen wickets and by talking with him during the intervals. In his first match W. G., not yet quite sixteen, made 32 against the bowling of such heroes as Tarrant, Tinley and Jackson. In 1865, aged sixteen, he was playing both at Lord's and the Oval for the Gentlemen against the Players. By profession Grace was a Gloucestershire doctor, but cricket was his life. Born in 1848, he survived until 1915 and played until he was sixty, when he took to golf and bowls. His first lessons in the game were from his mother, but he had an elder brother, E. M., known as 'The Coroner', born in 1841, whose example and enthusiasm must have meant much to the youthful paragon. E. M. was a forceful and opportunist bat, very wily with the ball, and the best point of his time, earning him the nickname of 'the Policeman' from Tom Emmett, the Yorkshire fast bowler, an incorrigible wag. The modern first-class game knows the place 'at the point of the bat' no longer: a strange case of evolution. E. M. was so active that he is said once to have caught out a man at square-leg off his own bowling.

From the time of his début onwards, W. G.'s career of conquest was steady in every department of the game: batting, bowling, fielding and captaincy. One of his maxims which should never be forgotten was 'Go for the bowling before it goes for you'; and that he himself obeyed it there are abundant and glorious proofs, not least his famous innings of 288 against Somersetshire in May, 1895, his forty-seventh year, when we have the evidence of the Rev. A. P. Wickham, the Somersetshire wicket-keeper, that during this feat of endurance and skill the Champion allowed only four balls to pass him. Among the bowlers was S. M. J. Woods, some of whose balls were bumpers, too.

No other great batsman matured so early and so swiftly as W. G., until three or four years ago when Don Bradman, the young Australian, arose to set the best bowlers of both hemispheres the hardest problem of their time. Whether Bradman will develop into another W. G. only those with long lives before them will see. Meanwhile he stands as the most remarkable young batsman of our day, with perfect defence and every scoring stroke.

W. G.'s true successor, however, is J. B., or 'Jack', Hobbs, the idol of the Oval, whose defence and attack and knowledge of running made him the world's finest batsman and kept him in that position for many years. He was also the best cover-point, with the quickest and truest return to the wicket.

During W. G.'s reign practically all the strokes, as distinguished from hits, had come in, to be developed and enriched and refined until in the 1890's they reached their complete range and perfection of execution in the hands of an Indian youth, Kumar Shri Ranjitsinhji, known to the world as 'Ranji' and now, in his maturity, the ruler of Nawanagar. Whatever has happened in batting since Ranjitsinhji's prime has merely been different according to the idiosyncrasy of the player. W. G. did more for cricket as a whole, and was a bowler too; but I look upon Ranjitsinhji as the greatest virtuoso of sheer batsmanship, and not very far below him are Victor Trumper, C. G. Macartney, and Jack Hobbs. Victor Trumper died, still young, in 1915; Macartney has retired from the first-class game, but Hobbs, although born as long ago as 1882, is still (1933) doing wonderful things.

In the space of a brief survey such as this, I cannot hope to do justice to all the great players of Grace's time and after. I must therefore confine myself to the giants, and I take them in the order of their birth; beginning with 1849, in order to include Mr. W. Yardley of Cambridge (he made two

W. G. GRACE

hundreds in the University match) and Kent, who
was a very dangerous bat and could bowl with both
arms: fast round with his right and lobs with his
left.   The year 1850 brought into the world R. G.
Barlow, the Lancashire stone-waller (whom I must
couple with his captain and senior by three years,
Mr. A. N. Hornby, the stealer of runs); George
Ulyett, the genial Yorkshire all-rounder, who made
what has been described as the most sensational
catch in the history of the game; F. Morley, the
Notts fast bowler; Mr. C. I. Thornton, of Kent and
Middlesex, the mighty hitter; Mordecai Sherwin,
the Notts wicket-keeper; William Barnes, the Notts
all-rounder; Louis Hall, the Yorkshire batsman,
a model of patience; F. R. Spofforth, the Australian
demon bowler; J. Crossland, the Lancashire fast
bowler; Alec Bannerman, the Australian stone-
waller; the Rev. Vernon Royle, of Lancashire, the
best cover-point ever known; Willy Bates, the
Yorkshire all-rounder; W. L. Murdoch, the Australian captain; Mr. W. W. Read, the Surrey batsman;
Mr. A. J. Webbe, the Middlesex captain; J. McC.
Blackham, the Australian wicket-keeper; G. J.
Bonnor, the Australian giant and hitter; Dick
Pilling, the Lancashire wicket-keeper; Wilfrid
Flowers, the Notts all-rounder; Arthur Shrewsbury,
the Notts maker of centuries without a flaw; W.
Scotton, the Notts breaker of bowlers' hearts;

Edward Peate, the Yorkshire bowler; the Hon. Alfred Lyttelton, the Middlesex wicket-keeper; Bobby Peel, the Yorkshire bowler; William Gunn, the Notts batsman; Mr. A. G. Steel, the Cambridge and Lancashire all-rounder; George Giffen, the Australian all-rounder and one of the greatest names in the game; the Hon. Ivo Bligh, afterwards Lord Darnley, the Kent batsman and out-field; Maurice Read, the Surrey batsman and out-field; R. Abel, the Surrey batsman; Mr. C. T. Studd, the Cambridge and Middlesex all-rounder; W. Attewell, the Notts bowler who never lost his length; Sir T. C. O'Brien, the Oxford and Middlesex late-cutter; Johnny Briggs, the Lancashire bowler, batsman and mid-off; C. T. B. Turner, the Australian bowler; Allen Hill, the Yorkshire fast bowler; J. J. Lyons, the Australian hitter; Mr. H. T. Hewett, the Oxford and Somerset left-handed smiter; Mr. A. E. Stoddart, the Middlesex captain, mid-off and England batsman; George Lohmann, the Surrey all-rounder; A. Mold, the Lancashire fast bowler; Albert Ward, the Lancashire batsman; Mr. F. G. J. Ford, the Middlesex left-hander, who sent the ball to the boundary as though he were merely caressing the pitch; J. Tunnicliffe, the Yorkshire batsman and slip; G. H. S. Trott, the Australian captain; J. T. Hearne, the Middlesex medium-pace bowler; E. J. Tyler, the Somerset slow bowler; A. A. Lilley, the Warwick-

shire wicket-keeper; J. J. Ferris, the Australian and
Gloucestershire bowler; H. Trumble, the Australian
bowler; Mr. S. M. J. Woods, the Cambridge and
Somersetshire all-rounder; W. H. Lockwood, the
Surrey fast bowler; Mr. Gregor McGregor, the Cam-
bridge and Middlesex captain and wicket-keeper; W.
Mead, the Essex bowler; the Hon. F. S. Jackson, the
Cambridge and Yorkshire all-rounder; Mr. L. C. H.
Palairet, the Oxford and Somersetshire batsman, as
graceful as Pilch and Daft; J. Darling, the Australian
captain; Tom Richardson, the Surrey fast bowler;
Tom Hayward, the Surrey batsman; G. H. Hirst, the
Yorkshire all-rounder; Mr. A. C. Maclaren, the Lancashire captain and batsman; Mr. C. J. Kortright, the
Essex fast bowler; Schofield Haigh, the Yorkshire
fast bowler; Mr. C. B. Fry, the Oxford and Sussex
scientific batsman; Mr. A. O. Jones, the Nottinghamshire captain and slip; K. S. Ranjitsinhji, the superb,
of whom I have spoken earlier; M. A. Noble, the
Australian captain and all-rounder, one of the finest
cricketers of all; John Tyldesley, the Lancashire
batsman and out-field; Tom Wass, the Notts fast
bowler; Mr. H. D. G. Leveson-Gower, of Oxford and
Surrey, one of the pillars of the game; Mr. P. F.
Warner, the Middlesex and England captain; Albert
Trott, the gallant all-rounder who came to Middlesex
from Australia and once hit a ball over Lord's
pavilion; J. T. Brown, of Yorkshire, who invented

the hook stroke; David Denton, of Yorkshire, the
batsman and out-field; Mr. G. L. Jessop, the hurri-
cane hitter and all-rounder, of Cambridge, Gloucester-
shire and England; Mr. J. R. Mason, the Kentish
all-rounder; Joe Vine, the Sussex out-field; L. C.
Braund, the Somersetshire all-rounder; R. O.
Schwarz, the South African all-rounder; Mr. W.
Brearley, the Lancashire fast bowler; Mr. P. A.
Perrin, the Essex batsman; John Gunn, the Notts slow
bowler; Mr. B. J. T. Bosanquet, the perfector of
English googlies; Clem Hill, Australia's left-hander;
Wilfrid Rhodes, the Yorkshire all-rounder and best
slow bowler since William Lillywhite; Victor
Trumper, the Australian, to whose genius I have
already referred; Mr. R. E. Foster, of Worcestershire,
most illustrious of many Foster brothers; W. W.
Armstrong, the slow bowler and Australian captain;
George Gunn, of Notts, a master batsman; Colin
Blythe, the Kent slow bowler and one of the best in
the whole long tradition; Mr. K. L. Hutchings who,
like Blythe, was killed in the War and was promising
to be the most forceful bat of his day; Mr. R. H.
Spooner, of Lancashire, another master; P. W. Sher-
well, the South African wicket-keeper and captain;
Harry Strudwick, the Surrey wicket-keeper; J.
Hardstaff, the Nottinghamshire batsman and out-
field; J. B. Hobbs of Surrey and numberless Tests,
of whom I have spoken; W. Bardsley, the Aus-

tralian batsman; A. Cotter, the Australian fast bowler; C. W. L. Parker, the Gloucestershire slow bowler, unplayable on soft wickets; C. G. Macartney, the Australian all-rounder and one of the greatest geniuses of cricket; A. Ducat, the Surrey batsman; H. T. W. Hardinge, the Kentish all-rounder; J. W. Hitch, the Surrey fast bowler and incomparably courageous field; C. P. Mead, of Hants, the dogged left-hander; W. W. Whysall, of Notts, the batsman; P. Holmes, who goes in first for Yorkshire with Sutcliffe; F. E. Woolley, the Kent and England all-round left-hander, in whose powerful but effortless hands the bat looks like a toy; A. P. Freeman, of Kent, one of the most dangerous of slow bowlers, although only a few inches high; E. Hendren, of Middlesex, batsman, long-field, short-slip and famous thrower-in; Roy Kilner, of Yorkshire, the all-rounder; A. Sandham, of Surrey, who goes in first with Hobbs and often stays there longer; J. W. Hearne, the Middlesex all-rounder; and Mr. J. C. White, of Somerset and England, the slow bowler. We have now reached 1891.

The next ten years gave the cricket field Mr. P. G. H. Fender, the Surrey all-rounder; C. V. Grimmett, the Australian slow bowler; G. Geary, the Leicestershire fast bowler; Herbert Sutcliffe, of Yorkshire, who goes in first for England and by his fielding converts boundary hits into singles; W. A.

Oldfield, the Australian wicket-keeper, and W. M. Woodfull, the Australian captain; Maurice Tate, the Sussex and England bowler and cheerful hitter; Richard Tyldesley, the Lancastrian slow bowler; J. O'Connor, the Essex batsman; Mr. A. P. F. Chapman, the Kentish and England captain and a fieldsman of almost magical powers; Maurice Leyland, the Yorkshire left-handed all-rounder; G. Duckworth, the England and Lancashire wicker-keeper; Mr. R. E. S. Wyatt, the Warwickshire and England captain and all-rounder; and the Australian fast bowler, J. M. Gregory (nephew of S. E. Gregory), whose bumping deliveries had caused Test match batsmen to lower their heads long before Larwood was heard of. If I extended the birth qualification to 1905 we should get Walter Hammond, of Gloucestershire, the best of the younger all-rounders of the day, and K. S. Duleepsinhji, the Sussex captain and the most accomplished and adventurous of the younger batsmen. The Infant Phenomenon of Australia, Don Bradman, was not born till 1908.

And lastly let me mention the two cricketing peers who have done so much for the modern game: the late Lord Harris, of Eton, Oxford and Kent and in 1895 President of the M.C.C., who was not only a very live cricketer for most of his days, taking part annually in a Fourth of June game at Eton until he was an octogenarian, but a zealous worker for cricket all the world over; and Lord Hawke, of Eton, Cambridge and Yorkshire, who was captain of his usually triumphant county for many years, from 1914 to 1918 was President of the M.C.C. and happily is still with us.   Lord Harris and Lord Hawke may be called the modern representatives of the third Duke of Dorset, who did so much for cricket nearly two hundred years ago.   Such enthusiasm and interest are particularly admirable when one reflects that cricket has always been a democratic game without respect of persons: noblemen get no preferential treatment even on their own village grounds.

I have written elsewhere—obliquely—of how, when I was very young, I was engaged, in the Brighton cricket pavilion, in a small wager with A. N. Hornby.   Since then I have known personally many illustrious performers, but the first that I often met was, in the same ground, J. W. Juniper, the fast left-hand Sussex bowler.   When, as a Brighton schoolboy in 1880 and 1881, I had the run of the county ground, where we had for our matches a section at the north-east corner, Juniper was one of our heroes and we used to supply him with shandygaff or beer at Host Juden's bar. Juniper was familiarly known as 'Jumper' for the reason, I believe, that very few people can write the word Juniper without a compositor misreading it. Although 'Jumper' was in those days a guileless, graceless, happy-go-lucky creature of nineteen or twenty, in fact very little older than we were, only the boldest—such is the complex nature of the hero-worshipper—dared to address him by his nickname. I can acutely recall how day after day I determined at last to call him 'Jumper', but again found such ease with the great an impossibility and once more declined meekly to formality. 'Mr. Juniper, your very good health.'

If 'Jumper' was the object of our affection we kept a totally different set of emotions for another habitué of Host Juden's bar, the ground-man, Nathaniel Burchell, who was never our guest and who I am bound to say behaved accordingly. To him every boy was an actual or potential ball-stealer, whereas to the genial 'Jumper' every boy was a possible entertainer. 'Jumper' had only one eye, the other having been destroyed by a branch which sprang back from someone preceding him in a coppice. The loss may have been the reason why his batting was so unlike that of Don Bradman; but it made no difference to his bowling, which could be very deadly. Why he died at so early an age—only twenty-three—I do not remember, but most cordially hope it was not the result of his young admirers' hospitality. I am led, however, to fear so, from the far superior longevity of Burchell.

How to explain the fascination that cricket exerts? It is not simple. That it should attract the proficients is understandable, although they are liable to continual mischances and mortifications such as no other game presents; but the curious thing is that it attracts the incompetents as well; those who never make a run, and cannot bowl, and yet, doomed only to dreary waiting in the pavilion and to fatiguing fielding, turn up punctually on every occasion, hoping for the best, and even (such is the human heart's buoyancy) expecting it. There is no other game at which the confirmed duffer is so persistent and so undepressed. It is for the experts, victims of misfortune, that depression waits; it is they who chew the cud of bitterness.

The phrase about 'the glorious uncertainty of cricket' applies to the individual as much as to the fortunes of the struggle. For there is no second chance: the batsman who is out first ball must retire to the pavilion and brood on his ill-luck until it is time to field and forget it—when, as likely as not, he will miss a catch and enter purgatory again. The lawn-tennis player, no matter how badly he is playing, completes the set; the footballer, no matter how inept, kicks again; the polo player and the hockey player, though covered with shame, are assured of their full afternoon's sport. But it may

8

easily be the best batsman's fate to have nothing to do but watch more fortunate batsmen receiving easier bowling than he did. This constant risk of making no runs would, you would think, deflect boys and men from the game. But no. The cricketing temperament, always slightly sardonic, accepts it. The uncertainty spells also glory.

There is also, still further to nourish this sardonic tendency, the weather. No game depends more upon friendly atmospheric conditions, and no game therefore is so frequently spoiled. One wonders sometimes if England may not have had a totally different climate when cricket was chosen as its national summer game; for one reads little of rain in the accounts of early matches. Were we to choose again should we again select cricket? The answer, I am sure, is yes, so undefeatable is our optimism; but surely there are more clouds than there used to be?

The conditions of the game are unique and fascinating. No other game lasts so long: Test matches are often played to a finish; first-class matches are spread over three days of changing fortunes which every ball may affect; the village match occupies four or five hours, equally packed with drama. If it is exciting to watch the ups and downs of these struggles, where the proverbial glorious uncertainty of the game is ever present, think what it must be to be one of the two-and-twenty participants.   And under propitious skies how benign are the circumstances of the struggle! The sun shines, the turf is warm and scented.   But perhaps, when all is said, the secret of the spell of cricket lies in the possibilities of every ball.   The bat awaiting the ball is indeed an implement of destiny, but the ball which the bat awaits is more fateful.   In its flight through the air, after it has left the bowler's hand and before it reaches the batsman, the spectator can live a lifetime.

The mechanics of cricket are, I imagine, now fixed.   There will be no new strokes; no new varieties of bowling; all that the lawgivers of the M.C.C. will have to do in the future is to deal with minor details and the politics and finance of the game: the control of Test teams, the county championship and so forth.   But these are trifles. Let us do honour to the giants, let us go to see them when we ourselves are past playing and even when we are young and emulous; but gate-money cricket remains spectacular and apart.   Cricket is not the county ground, although that may be the Heaven on which every boy's eyes are fixed; cricket is the backyard, the garden, the playground, the school-field, the club and college ground, and, above all, the village green.

'Oh,' wrote an old enthusiast to me during the

period of strife at Adelaide early in this year (not of Grace) 1933; 'Oh, all this psychology! I like better the local match on a small ground where all the better balls were hit into the hayfield and lost. In despair a pudding was produced and a hefty butcher smote it so violently that he knocked the cover clean off it. The cover was caught by the wicket-keeper, but the core was missed by point. And the deuce and all arose. Was he out or not? I say he wasn't, putting the case before the cover. But never mind—that's cricket, and it's the reason why the game will always be loved in spite of journalists and prizes to readers. There's something about cricket that defeats snobs and conquers the press-gang. It's a lovely game, is now and ever will be.'

Should every county ground be closed and never another shilling of gate-money leave our pockets, cricket would still be in England's lifeblood, drawing its undismayable devotees from every section of the nation: the cricket that has such a hold on the young that they take their bats to bed with them, and on the old that they cannot see half a dozen urchins in the street, with only a lamp-post for stumps, without pausing for a minute or two to watch; the cricket that stirs up such a turmoil of hopes and fears in our breasts that to consult the barometer can be almost an anguish.

JOHN NYREN

'Upon a Hampshire hill-top
  Beside the "Bat and Ball",
Old Richard Nyren nurtured
  The noblest game of all.

The daisies lost their pretty heads
  When David Harris bowled;
The stumps were two, the bats were curved;
  But ah, the Age of Gold!'

THE large room in the Pavilion at Lord's
—the room in which members walk about
behind the bowler's arm until the umpire
stops them—contains one of the most interesting
collections of pictures in the world. It is, of
course, not complete; it could not be complete
when the Pavilion at the Oval has the George Mor-
land; but it has recently reached a point nearer perfection by the addition of a portrait of John Nyren,
because John Nyren was the son of Richard Nyren,
the mainspring of the Hambledon Club, where,
as I have been trying to explain, first-class cricket
received its best nourishment, and later in life he
was the author of an early practical guide to the

game, *The Young Cricketer's Tutor*, which, after the instructive part is over, burgeons into those vital, racy character sketches of good men and true entitled 'Cricketers of My Time'. A portrait of John Nyren is as essential to Lord's as, say, at the Admiralty a portrait of Nelson, or at the Invalides a portrait of Napoleon—all capital N's and all, as it happens, contemporaries.

The picture in question, reproduced in this book, is of Kit-cat size, very sympathetically painted: the kind of portrait which looks as though it were a true likeness. It reached the M.C.C. through Miss Elizabeth Nyren, John Nyren's granddaughter, who (1933) is still living, in advanced years, at Hythe. There is no artist's signature and no date, but I think we may assume the sitter's age to be about fifty. In looking at it we should remember the description of Nyren written by Charles Cowden Clarke for the second edition of *The Young Cricketer's Tutor*, a deathless work which, but for him, would never have existed.

'Mr. Nyren', he says, 'was a remarkably well-grown man, standing nearly 6 feet, of large proportions throughout, big-boned, strong, and active. He had a bald, bullet head, a prominent forehead, small features, and little deeply-sunken eyes. His smile was as sincere as an infant's. If there were any deception in him, Nature herself was to blame in giving him those insignificant, shrouded eyes. They made no *show* of observation, but they were perfect ministers to their master. Not a thing, not a motion,

JOHN NYREN
From the Painting in the Pavilion at Lord's

escaped them in a company, however numerous. Here was one
secret of his eminence as a cricketer.'

Again:

'A more single and gentle hearted, and yet thoroughly manly,
man I never knew; one more forbearing towards the failings of
others, more unobtrusively steady in his own principles, more
cheerfully pious, more free from cant and humbug of every description. He possessed an instinctive admiration of everything
good and tasteful, both in Nature and art. He was fond of flowers,
and music, and pictures; and he rarely came to visit us without
bringing with him a choice specimen of a blossom, or some other
natural production, or a manuscript copy of an air which had
given him pleasure. And so, hand in hand with these simple
delights, he went on to the last, walking round his garden on the
morning of his death.'

Where John acquired his culture is something
of a mystery. All that he tells us is that a Jesuit
—the Nyrens were an old Catholic family—taught
him some Latin; and Hambledon, where he was
brought up, is, even now, not an educational centre.
Probably once again, as in the case of so many
illustrious men, we must seek the source in the
mother: Frances Pennicud, of Slindon, in Sussex,
a lady of Quaker origin. When, in 1906, I was
preparing my edition of *The Young Cricketer's Tutor*,
under the title *The Hambledon Men*, Miss Mary
Nyren, John's oldest granddaughter, wrote for
me some traditional notes of her great-grandmother.
Mrs. Richard Nyren, she said, was 'a friend of the

Countess of Newburgh, who gave her a large prayer-book, in which the names of her children were afterwards inscribed. When she was an old lady, still living at Hambledon, she dressed in a soft, black silk dress, with a large Leghorn hat tied on with a black lace scarf, and used a gold-headed cane when out walking. She went out only to church, and on errands of mercy. . . . Mrs. Nyren, when a widow, found a happy home in her son John Nyren's house till her death at over ninety years of age.'

The inference, I think, may safely be drawn that at his mother's knee John Nyren acquired some, at any rate, of his gentleness and taste.

This is not to belittle Richard Nyren, of whom I wish that we knew more, and who we may be sure was the boy's model in integrity and worth. His son gives him, indeed, a noble character:

'I never saw a finer specimen of the thoroughbred old English yeoman than Richard Nyren. He was a good, face-to-face, unflinching, uncompromising, independent man. He placed a full and just value upon the station he held in society, and he maintained it without insolence or assumption. He could differ with a superior, without trenching upon his dignity or losing his own. I have known him maintain an opinion with great firmness against the Duke of Dorset and Sir Horace Mann; when, in consequence of his being proved to be in the right, the latter has afterwards crossed the ground and shaken him heartily by the hand. Richard Nyren was a safe batsman and an excellent hitter. Although a

very stout man (standing about five feet nine) he was uncommonly
active. He owed all the skill and judgement he possessed to an
old uncle, Richard Newland, of Slindon, in Sussex, under whom
he was brought up—a man so famous in his time, that when a
song was written in honour of the Sussex cricketers, Richard Newland was especially and honourably signalized. . . . When Richard
Nyren left Hambledon, the club broke up, and never resumed
from that day. The head and right arm had gone.'

Nothing could be better and more direct than
that; but it is not enough, for according to Mr.
Haygarth, who wrote the biographies for *Lillywhite*, Richard Nyren gave up his farm to become
landlord of the 'Bat and Ball' on the edge of Broadhalfpenny Down, and no one who has seen that
somewhat squalid inn can believe that the distinguished Frances Nyren and her family could
have lived there; for it is merely a small beer-house
which any promoted potman could have run. Is it
possible, you ask yourself, that Richard Nyren, the
General of the Hambledon Club and the sturdy
companion of the nobility and aristocracy, was
landlord here? Later, says Mr. Haygarth, Richard
Nyren took the George in Hambledon village: a
larger inn, with stabling and a bedroom or two,
but still not a home for a highly respected Catholic
farmer and his fastidious Quaker wife.

Miss Mary Nyren, speaking, of course, only
from family tradition, for she could have known
nothing of her great-grandfather and very little of

her grandfather, denied the innkeeping altogether, stating as her belief that the Boniface Nyren, if a member of the family at all, was possibly John's elder brother Richard, but probably another man of the same name; and when one considers that John Nyren never hints that his father (the 'King Arthur of the Hambledon round table', as he calls him) was associated with the vending of the glorious Hambledon punch and ale of which he sings the praises in a passage too well known to quote in full —punch that would make a cat speak, ale that would put the souls of three butchers into one weaver—I am disposed to agree with her. Surely if these divine liquors and the accompanying viands had been of his father's dispensing John would have been proud to say so. I must not be thought a detractor of publicans. Far from it. I rejoice in their ministrations. And where would Nottinghamshire cricket be if William Clarke had not been the landlord of the inn at Trent Bridge? I am merely suggesting that there has been some confusion, and that so long as he was at Hambledon John Nyren's father remained a 'proud yeoman', more than a little bored during the months of October, November, December, January, February, March, and early April, as I hope and feel sure his son was, too.

Born on his father's farm at Hambledon in

Hampshire in 1764, John became a member of the
Club at the height of its fame, in 1778, and was
useful to it until 1791, when his father, then nearly
sixty, moved to London.   Of his own performances
as a 'farmer's pony'—his own phrase—he says
nothing, the only reference to any innings in which
he took part being where he mentions the move
from Broadhalfpenny Down, now commemorated
by a granite monument, to Windmill Down, which
was preferred for the odd reason, from the modern
point of view, that 'the ground declined every way
from the centre', thus, for very self-protection,
forcing watchfulness and agility on the fieldsmen.
So much did it slope, Nyren tells us, that once,
when he was in with Noah Mann, that impetuous
gipsy hit a ball behind him for which they ran ten.

We know more of John's own cricket in his
post-Hambledon period.   In the same year, 1791,
in which Richard Nyren moved to London, John
married and settled at Portsea, his wife being Miss
Cleopha Copp, a lady of German extraction with
a competency of her own.   From Portsea they
moved to Bromley in Middlesex, then to Battersea,
then to a house in Cheyne Walk, and finally to
Bromley again.   Nyren's business was calico-print-
ing, but he did not allow it to interfere with the
real purpose of life, for in 1796 he joined the
famous Homerton Club, which afterwards was to

amalgamate with the M.C.C. The Hambledon records do not allow us to distinguish between father and son, as no initial is given, until 1787, when *Lillywhite's Scores and Biographies* credits J. Nyren with 3 and 1 for Hambledon against England, while in 1788 for Hampshire against Surrey at Moulsey Hurst he made 3 and 9, falling both times to a ball from his old Hambledon colleague, the dreaded Lumpy; but from 1801 to 1808 John's appearances in the first-class game are carefully noted. At Lord's, for instance, on 25th August, 1802, playing for England against Surrey, he was bowled for 0 in his first innings by his Hambledon friend, Tom Walker, and in his second innings, after making 30, by Harry Walker, the other of the two 'anointed clod-stumpers'. As a fieldsman he was famous for his courage at the point of the bat, taking balls (says his son) that might have been discharged from a cannon. Against Twenty-two of Surrey at Lord's on 6, 7, 8, 9 and 10 June, 1803, he caught six. In 1804, for Homerton (with Beldham, Nyren's Hambledon hero, 'Silver Billy') against the M.C.C., he made 23 and 40, and in 1808 he made for Homerton 24 and 10, being bowled by the reverend but very short-tempered Lord Frederick Beauclerk in the first innings and by Silver Billy in the second, and catching out four. His last first-class match was

in 1817, when he was fifty-three, playing for Lord
Frederick's side against a team brought together
by the illustrious Mr. William Ward, to whom
Nyren later was to dedicate his book. But this
time, alas! he failed to score. Lambert was also
playing in the match and so was Mr. George
Osbaldeston, famous in every sporting circle as
'The Squire'. We should know far more of John
Nyren, and also of the Hambledon Club, had there
not in 1825 been a fire at Lord's in which valuable
early records of the game were destroyed.

After cricket, Nyren's chief enthusiasm was for
music, which he played, as a violinist, as well as
being in a small way a composer. In my book
The Hambledon Men I reproduce his setting of
a drinking song by Lord Byron. His principal
musical friend was Vincent Novello, with whom he
was associated for thirteen years at St. Mary's,
Moorfields, where Novello was organist and Nyren
choir-master. At Novello's 'Sunday Evenings',
which Charles Lamb has made historic in an Elia
essay, he was a regular attendant, while with the
family he was a special favourite. Oddly enough
it was through his intimacy with the Novellos that
he came to be the author of his cricket classic, for
one of the Novello girls, Mary, had married a
young literary man named Charles Cowden Clarke,
a schoolfellow of Keats and friend of Lamb, and

it was Clarke, so we must suppose, who, attracted by the old man's vivid cricket talk, persuaded him to let him make a book of it. Hence *The Young Cricketer's Tutor*, by John Nyren, to which is added *The Cricketers of My Time: or Recollections of the Most Famous Old Players*, by the same author, 'the whole collected and edited by Charles Cowden Clarke', 1833. According to Clarke, the book was 'compiled from unconnected scraps and reminiscences during conversation', while his widow, writing many years later, says that Nyren 'used to come and communicate his cricketing experiences to Charles'. Since Charles never wrote independently anything with the gusto of these inimitable pages, and since the only unassisted prose that I can find with Nyren's name to it is insipid, we must assume that Nyren as a talker had great gifts of liveliness and vigour, and that Clarke was artist enough to recognize them and reproduce them faithfully. Without Clarke, Nyren's book could not be; without Nyren, Clarke would never have thought of cricket as a theme for his pen. The fruit of their collaboration is a piece of literature as honest and glowing as any in the language.

THE SPIRE OF ENGLAND

TO say that Salisbury Cathedral has a spire is inexcusably to understate the case; it has *the* spire. Spires pierce the sky all over the country, some, such as Grantham's, seeming to be higher than anything we have ever seen; but Salisbury's surpasses them all, and, furthermore, is the most beautiful. It has yet another distinction in being the subject of the only joke on a church spire made by Charles Lamb, who, hearing that a party of friends had picnicked at its summit, remarked that 'they must have been sharp-set'.

To come to figures, Salisbury's spire is four hundred feet (the last three or four of which are out of the perpendicular); and one of the excitements of approaching the city by road, from whatever quarter, is the first glimpse of it, usually over the shoulder of a hill. 'There it is!' we exclaim. 'Look! The spire!' Thus, in France, does one glimpse, above the cornfields, the towers of Chartres.

Before there was Salisbury, or New Sarum, there was Old Sarum, and no one must think he knows anything of Salisbury until he has roamed about the strange pyramidal hill, a mile or so north of the city, which once was Old Sarum, and has made there some effort to reconstruct the past. To my mind the ruins of Old Sarum present problems more interesting than those of Stonehenge; and every day the excavations carried out under the Office of Works reveal new evidences of the extent and splendour of the fortress and the cathedral: the feudal system in essence.

To most people Old Sarum is a joke, a single farmhouse which for many years, until the passing of the Reform Act in 1832, returned two members to Parliament on behalf of the highest bidder. But before it had fallen into nothingness—and its decay and disappearance are among the most mysterious occurrences in English history—the place was popular and powerful. Although the Romans undoubtedly fortified it, historians think that the Britons had done so first. Under William the Conqueror a castle was built here and a cathedral was planned. It is conjectured that the castle with its keep and its surrounding towers was one of the largest in England, and the hill must have been a magnificent and imposing sight from any point of view, but particularly perhaps from the west, where the prospect would include the cathedral as well. The foundations of the cathedral are now clearly marked and much of the castle can be traced; but

SALISBURY CATHEDRAL FROM THE SOUTH-WEST

I wish that some imaginative architect would reconstruct the whole mound in a model such as you see of the Roman baths at Bath. It must, says the excellent little guide-book which the caretaker sells for sixpence, 'have been very similar in appearance to the towns so often seen on the Continent and especially in Italy, with their castles, churches, and houses perched in a closely united mass on the crest of some steeply-rising hill'.

This very congestion was the cause of Old Sarum's downfall. The Dean and Chapter of the Cathedral petitioned the Pope to let them move into the valley. They gave various reasons: as that the proximity of the cathedral to the castle was dangerous to life; that the place was windy and rheumatic; that the sun was so bright on the chalk that many of the clerks were blinded; that water had to be bought and brought from a distance; that the garrison there exerted anything but an influence for good; and so forth. And thus, the prayer being heeded, the new cathedral, down near the river, far from a licentious soldiery and sheltered from the weather, was in 1220 begun, and after 1227 the cathedral on the hill was abandoned. Many of the actual stones from the old fane were, however, employed in the building of the new, so that the two Sarums commingle.

The castle lasted longer, but in the fifteenth

9

century it, too, became derelict, and any one who
wanted its material might have it. To-day, under
the fostering care of the Office of Works, it is an
eloquent husk, speaking movingly of the past,
and offering, for those who can climb, fine views
of the low-lying riverside city which has supplanted
it and of the surrounding country.

One reads in the guide-books about the harm
caused to the new Salisbury cathedral by the changes
and renovations of James Wyatt, a seventeenth-
century architect known as 'The Destroyer'; but
it is good enough for me. Externally and internally
it has a beauty that can bring a lump to the throat,
and especially am I moved as I first enter and see
the miraculous black and white clustered columns
mounting upwards to the roof like the stalks of
lilies, many flowers making one; for more than
any other this cathedral has a flowerlike effect,
such is its grace and its light and its almost unbe-
lievable delicacy. Stone has been made to do more
than one could expect from it. Never can atmospheric space have been so radiantly shaped and
enclosed.

There is, indeed, almost too much for the eye;
for after the glories of the cathedral there is still
the dazzling beauty of the Chapter-house, with its
aerial roof springing from one central column and
its filagree walls of glass. Coming suddenly into

it from the grey and green quietude of the cloisters is almost to receive a blow.

Round the walls of the Chapter-house is a carved frieze representing the earlier incidents of the Old Testament, beginning with the creation of Adam; passing on to the drama of the Garden of Eden (note how happy is Eve to be clasping in her arms the little Cain); and so, through the Flood and the romantic history of Joseph, to Moses on Sinai embracing that embarrassing burden, the Ten Commandments; and so the summary ends.

According to a Shropshire rhyme, Clunbury, Clunton, and Clun are the quietest places under the sun; but I think I should give my vote to the Close of Salisbury Cathedral, where there are great expanses of lawn, ancient trees, houses large and small but all distinguished and desirable and in every style of English architecture from Tudor onwards, rules against admitting dogs except on a lead, and everywhere the stillness generated and diffused by the spire. A jackdaw may now and then dare to utter a cry, a pigeon venture to coo; but the silence is rarely broken, and one is conscious of the ecclesiastical past brooding over all. Salisbury, busy, noisy, full of pork-butchers and eating-houses, motor-cars and trippers, is just outside the walls; but it only washes up to them: the Close is as far from the ordinary citizen as though it were on foreign soil.

I never saw gathered together so many attractive English homes, from mansion to cottage (one of them a most impudent encroachment), as those which surround Salisbury's cathedral both in the Close and its tributaries, the abodes, I take it, chiefly of the clergy, although King's House, through whose mullioned windows you see the garden beyond, is a college for school-mistresses. The Bishop's Palace, with its smooth turf and its flowers and its cedars, just to the south of the cathedral, is probably the most delectable of all, but the ordinary stranger cannot see it. Were it not for the overpowering continuous presence of the cathedral, I think there is no place where I would sooner lead the leisurely meditative life. But that spire would make me restive. It is unbearably omnipresent and awesome.

The most beautiful epitaph ever written on a tomb ought to be in Salisbury Cathedral; but it is not. The sympathetic and accomplished creature that it celebrates is buried there, with her kin, on the north side of the altar of the Lady Chapel; but there is no means of identifying the grave. Yet there, 'the subject of all verse', she lies: Mary Herbert, wife of the second Earl of Pembroke. How exquisite is the praise!—

'Underneath this sable hearse
Lies the subject of all verse:
Sidney's sister, Pembroke's mother.
Death, ere thou hast slain another,
Wise and fair and good as she,
Time shall throw a dart at thee.'

This lady, the Countess of Pembroke, who inspired her brother Philip Sidney's *Arcadia*, lived at Wilton, near Salisbury, and died there in 1621, and no one visiting Salisbury should forget to see this noble mansion—one of the few houses in England in which Shakespeare is known to have stayed, and a treasury of fine pictures and relics. The most famous of the Earls of Pembroke, William Herbert, the third Earl, the lover of Mary Fitton, and, according to many theorists, 'Mr. W. H.' himself, the 'onlie begetter' of Shakespeare's sonnets, was her son.

Every one who goes to Salisbury in the true spirit goes also to Bemerton, which is only a mile and a half beside the River Nadder, because it was there that holy Mr. Herbert was rector from 1630 till 1632, when he died at the early age of forty-two. One thinks of 'the sweetest singer that ever sang God's praise' as older than that. When not writing his poems and spreading piety and loving-kindness in his parish, Mr. Herbert used to walk into Salisbury to hear music in the cathedral and to join a party of friends in making it himself: a practice he would justify by saying that 'religion does not banish mirth, but only moderates and sets rules to it'.

Salisbury has another ecclesiastical link with literature in having sat for the Barchester of Trollope's novels of cathedral life. It was while he was at Salisbury in the course of an investigation for the General Post Office, where he was a clerk, that Trollope conceived the story of *The Warden*. 'I have been often asked', he wrote in his *Autobiography*, 'in what period of my early life I had lived so long in a cathedral city as to have become intimate with the ways of a Close. I never lived in any cathedral city. . . .' That a single midsummer evening's perambulation of the Close of Salisbury should lead to such a series of persuasive clerical annals is among the remarkable achievements of literature. For Hiram's Hospital, however, of which the Rev. Septimus Harding—'The Warden'—was in charge, Trollope, I fancy, went to Winchester, for the foundation is more similar to that of St. Cross than anything here.

A more vigorous writer than Trollope, and, in fact, the father of the English novel, Henry Fielding, is also associated with Salisbury. Not only did he occasionally live there, but it was at Salisbury that he found his first wife, Charlotte

SIGNBOARD OF THE OLD MILL INN AT WEST HARNHAM, NEAR SALISBURY
Painted by C. R. W. Nevinson

Cradock, the original of Amelia, even to the broken nose: the broken nose which, according to Dr. Johnson, 'spoilt the sale of perhaps the only book of which, printed off betimes one morning, a new edition was called for before night'.

Salisbury honours in the cathedral another writer as unlike, in different ways, Trollope and Fielding as could be imagined, but a master of English prose: Richard Jefferies, author of *The Story of My Heart*. The memorial is here less because of Jefferies' association with Salisbury than because he wrote largely of Wiltshire. His *Bevis*, a story for boys, has as its centre of excitement a lake at Coate, near Swindon, where Jefferies was born and brought up; his *Round about a Great Estate* is the description of Savernake and its forest, near Marlborough. Though I may seem to be digressing in my account of him, it is not so: in any book about England this lover of England should be extolled.

With the *Bevis* days the happiness of poor Jefferies was, I fear, over. Nature, which he worshipped with a white-hot passion, could not give him serenity of mind; and both the machinery of civilization, with its grinding need of money, and his own constant ill-health, were against him. He died at thirty-nine, an idealist, pantheist and rhapsodist, in an alien world, worn out by disease, overwork, and financial worry. When I visited his birthplace, a modest farmhouse behind a high wall at Coate, I noticed that the sign of the neighbouring inn was the 'Sun'. Could anything be more appropriate to the author of *The Story of My Heart*, with its insatiable craving for heat and life? The 'Sun'. A hundred yards from the farmhouse's back-door Jefferies could be at his beloved water's edge and among the animals that make up the microcosm of *Wood Magic*. Few solitary introspective boys with a naturalist's eyes can have had better conditions in which to grow thoughtful and observant.

It was after Jefferies' boyhood that tragedy set in. The escapade of his sixteenth year, when with a friend he ran away to France, may perhaps be called the end of irresponsibility. Their idea was to walk to Moscow, but as neither knew any foreign language they thought it better to change their route and go instead to America; but at Liverpool the cost of the tickets stopped further enterprise, and they returned by slow train to Swindon, depressed and disillusioned. The frustrated enterprise was symptomatic; for the rest of his life Richard Jefferies was to be short of cash and was to envisage seductive high roads leading towards delight but to be unable to take them.

On returning to his father's home, Coate Farm, he settled down to become a reporter for a Swindon paper, learning shorthand for the purpose; no career for such a dryad, nomad, and poet in one. In 1874 he married and devoted himself to writing novels, which had no success, for he lacked any sense of character; but in 1877, living in London, he came to his own with a series of articles in the *Pall Mall Gazette* called 'The Gamekeeper at Home', followed by 'Wild Life in a Southern County'— his native Wiltshire. *Wood Magic* and *Bevis* belong to 1881 and 1882, and *The Story of My Heart*, his most remarkable and individual work, to 1883. Fortune certainly played him strange tricks, for his next home was Brighton, whose treelessness he deplored in one of his essays. Brighton, however, like Glasgow, is a 'fine place to get away from', and in the neighbourhood he found materials for some of his most attractive essays. I remember, in particular, one called 'Clematis Lane', describing a spot near Patcham that I used to know well; in fact, all unconscious of his identity, I may have been loitering there at the same time.

Jefferies' last home was at Goring, also in Sussex, where he died in pain and poverty in 1887. His memorial, after his own books, is *The Eulogy of Richard Jefferies*, which Walter Besant, a sophisticated Londoner, turned aside from success as a novelist to write, and wrote with noble fervour, and this bust in Salisbury Cathedral, above a tablet stating how, 'observing the works of Almighty God with a poet's eye, he enriched the literature of his country and won for himself a place amongst those who have made men happier and wiser'. Alas, his own happiness was not too constant.

Salisbury is a meeting-place of the waters. Its principal river is the Avon, which in time will run into the sea at Christchurch Head. From the north-west comes the Wyly; from the west comes the Nadder; from the south-west comes the Ebble; from the north-east comes the Bourne. My advice to all visitors to Salisbury is to find their way sooner or later to West Harnham, south of the city, where there are two inns both of which afford a view of the spire of England. One is the 'Rose and Crown' and one 'The Old Mill,' the newly-painted sign of which I reproduce—both as a picture and as an indication of the efforts that are now being made, here and there all over the country, to give to inns a new dignity and charm.

I like, when I sit here, to think that John Constable sat here, too; as he must often have done, for Salisbury had a double attraction for him in its streams and in its cathedral. This, the great English impressionist landscape-painter (whose 'Hay Wain', exhibited in Paris in 1824, had so stimulating an effect on the French artists who saw it that the rise of the Barbizon school may be traced

STONEHENGE

to its influence), first visited Salisbury as the guest
of his friend, John Fisher, nephew of the John
Fisher who had been rector of Langham, Suffolk,
in what is now called the 'Constable country', and
who later was made Bishop of the Wiltshire see.
John Fisher the younger, who was his uncle's
chaplain, spread his belief in the genius of Constable near and far, and backed it by buying as
many of his pictures as he could afford. To the
circumstance that he was Constable's host we owe
not only the Salisbury scenes, notably that extraordinary feat of vivid brush-work, with the spire, the
river, and the bishop's garden, No. 2,651 in the
National Gallery, but also the magnificent 'Wey-
mouth Bay', with its luminous clouds: No. 2,652
in the same collection. How often Constable
painted the cathedral I cannot say, but again and
again, and always with an ecstatic splendour.

Although Stonehenge is ten miles from Salisbury,
we group it with the city—not a little from the
circumstance that of Salisbury Plain it is the special
glory. What was the purpose of this assemblage
of rocks, brought, it is known, from long distances,
no one can now for certain say; but the probabilities
are that Sir Norman Lockyer was right in con-
jecturing that Stonehenge was built as a temple
for solar observation, the crucial moment for the
observer being sunrise on the longest day. The

date of its erection he estimated at about 1600 B.C.,
a time at which the only astronomers in England
were the druidical priests. I quote Sir Norman's
words, which may, of course, be mistaken, but
which seem to me more reasonable than those of
other speculative investigators who would associate
these monoliths chiefly with sepulchral rites.

'It was absolutely essential for early man to know something
about the proper time for performing agricultural operations. We
now go into a shop, and for a penny buy our almanack which
gives us everything we want to know about the year, the month,
the day. But these poor people, unless they found out the times
of year for themselves, or got someone to tell them—and their
priests were the men who knew, and were priests *because* they
knew—had no means of determining when their various agricultural operations should take place, so that we find all over the
world temples erected in the very first flush of civilization.'

Stonehenge is not what it was even when Constable made his sinister picture, little more than a
century ago, for until quite recently, when protection set in, it was, like Old Sarum's cathedral and
castle, the resort of every one in the neighbourhood
who wanted free building material; but wisdom
comes in time, and this ancient temple can never
be harmed again, except by natural processes, for it
now belongs to the nation and is properly preserved.

The first view of Stonehenge has been known to
disappoint; the stranger has perhaps been expecting

too much. But let him make a habit of visiting Salisbury Plain at all seasons of the day and year, and he will realize the majesty and even sublimity of these tumbled monsters.

ON THE ROAD

THE sight the other day of a Breton carrying strings of onions with painful steps up one of the steep roads towards Ashdown Forest made me reflect on the long interval since I had last seen one of these intrepid foreign dispensers of the best of bulbs. (The best of lilies, I might have called it, but fear the wrath of those who say things with flowers.) Surely these Breton youths used to be very common objects of the country? I have the impression that one saw them continually in London and smaller towns, in couples, not distantly separated, one working along one side of the street and the other, the other, and then joining again. The onions, I am told, come from the neighbourhood of La Rochelle and old privileges are extended to the little ships that bring them and to the wayfaring pedlars, whose home capital is the little seaport of Roscoff in Brittany, and whose passports are readily granted even in these suspicious days. In Wales, it is said, they are easily understood—a lingual adjustment being arranged by the Celtic fringe—but elsewhere they employ the Volapuk of signs.

Foreign organ-grinders seem to have vanished completely—at any rate, the Italians whose head-quarters were in Saffron Hill and who were not without Simian allies. In fact, Jocko was the star performer. I rather fancy that the Duce had something to say about this industry, which reflected, he thought, upon the prestige of the new Italy: the Duce, who, I am convinced, would die happy, with all his other ambitions unfulfilled, if he could be assured that the word 'Wop' would never be used again. But they were gentle creatures, the Italian organ-grinders, with their little friends scampering up and down them, their olive faces and black hair and white smiling teeth and perpetual doffings of the hat; and, above all, with their unassertive melodies. I remember them as being so regular on their rounds that you could have set the clock by them. The German bands were regular, too, but not so modest with their music, which was mostly brass and was seldom in tune, but never, even when most dis-arranged, as offensive and cacophonous as the modern saxophonist and trap drummer can be. The German bands faded out, for very definite reasons, in 1914, and our street music is now supplied chiefly by ex-soldiers and is without any special character.

Not only was there the German band with its unmistakable tempo, but now and then—a rarer

visitant but far more thrilling—came the one-man
band: a man loaded not with mischief but melody,
or at any rate with the materials of melody, which,
when they were being played, brought into action
every muscle in his brave body.   So far as I can
remember, the drum-stick with which he belaboured
the sheepskin was fixed to his elbow; the crash of
cymbals involved a kick; when he shook his head a
hatful of bells rang out.

The organ-grinder with his monkey led, in one
family that I know, to a phrase, very cryptic to
strangers, which, although it originated nearly sixty
years ago, is still in use.   To this regular visitant the
mistress of the house was in the habit, every Friday
morning, of sending out a thick sandwich cut by
her own hands.   The circumstance that none of the
other itinerants received such an attention was noted
by the master of the house, who did his best to find
out why but was met always with evasion.   Hence
came the question 'What's the monkey man?'
signifying 'What is the mysterious meaning of all
this?'   And even now, on all occasions where
perplexity and curiosity join hands, 'What's the
monkey man?' is the form of words employed.

A more exciting and more erratic visitor than the
organ-grinder was the man with the dancing bear.
It is long since I saw one, and possibly he is for-
bidden by law, although it would have been more

logical to forbid him in the old horse days that I am recalling than now, when there is so little for him to frighten. I have seen horses stop and shiver as they entered the aura of these shaggy monsters; but the motor-car is made of sterner stuff. (As to the way of a steed with an elephant, when a circus procession came into the town—of course, the most magical of all our experiences, but very, very rare— an American novel has recently been published with the whole trouble in its title: *Hold Yer Hosses: The Elephants Are Coming!*) The bear had a rope round his neck, held by the man (who hailed, I fancy, from Russia or the Near East), and the man carried a long pole. We used to get as near as we dared, always perhaps a little equine in our attitude, and watch the poor clumsy creature hopping heavily from one foot to the other, until, the hat coming round, we prudently retired. They were always moving on, both the men with the bears and the Bretons with onions; no one knew where they slept.

The hot-chestnut man had to be sought for at the street corner, and so had the hot-potato man. But the muffin man went out into the open spaces, with his bell and his tray. He still, I suppose, may be heard, but it is long since the sound of his approach fell upon these enraptured ears. Sunday afternoon was his special time, and directly the blessed notes came over the air one of us, primed with the neces-

10

sary funds, would run out to intercept him: an important manœuvre, because the tray on his head, beneath its green baize cover, could hold only a limited supply, and other messengers, wholly unashamed of their greed, were also hurrying his way. It was an anxious time, I can tell you, and more than once I have had to return empty-handed and face an unreasonable and implacable household.   There is no fury like a muffin-eater disappointed.   I say muffin, but as a matter of fact the family to which I belonged were crumpet addicts, and to this day I should make crumpets—could I ever see them again—my first choice.

So far I have been recalling only the entertainers; but there was an occasional and official visitor who appealed to another sense than seeing and hearing— at any rate, in my own case—and this was the municipal water-cart.   We saw it only in summer, and only during droughts, when it arrived to lay the dust.   Tarmac being now the rule, what can the modern child know of the joy of following a water-cart just out of range of the jets and inhaling the exquisite scent made by the instantaneous mingling of the two elements?

I should have difficulty in saying when I last saw a water-cart sprinkling authentic dust, when I last saw a dancing bear, when I last saw a circus procession with, in the distance, finer and more resplend-

ent and more mountainous cars serenely rumbling our
way; but the other day a clown on stilts, one of the
essential accessories of these parades, was directing
the traffic in Leicester Square.   What now takes the
place of these old itinerants?   Who is the wandering
visitor to the small street and the country road to
make the childish heart beat faster?   I suppose it is
the Stop-me man on his tricycle.   Not that vendors
of ice-cream are a new institution, but they have
become more adventurous.   In my childhood there
were many ice-cream men, chiefly Italians, but they
were to be found at fixed points, purveying their
pink and white delicacies in little glasses, at a penny
or even a halfpenny each, which you licked thought-
fully and while licking contracted an ache at the
back of the eyes.   The conical cardboard receptacle
had not then been invented, although some genius
had just begun to wrap up an alluring slab of vanilla-
flavoured frigidity in a paper cover under the name
of Hokey Pokey.   (I regret to say my dictionary
basely relates this to Hocus Pocus; but a more
generous theory derives the words from the phrase
'Ecco   un   poco'   with   which   the   ingratiating
Southerner used to proffer his wares.   No child
of any intelligence would fail very quickly to get
'Hokey Pokey' out of that.)
   I remember that the Hokey Pokey men—probably because they were new-comers and could not

infringe upon vested rights—were less static than the others, and thus were the predecessors of the Stop-me man, although with a more restricted gambit. This must be so, or I should not have been told recently by the Lady Bountiful of a Sussex village that it has now become much more difficult to entertain and satisfy the various parties she is in the habit of giving—Sunday-school treats, harvest homes, mothers' meetings, and the like—because, whereas once upon a time there was no article of refreshment that, being in their lives so rare, was so eagerly anticipated and appreciated as ice-cream, they now think nothing of it at all. The Stop-me man has turned a luxury into a commonplace.

ENGLAND'S SPA

BATH may not be a bee, but she is a very beautiful drone. There is certainly no inland town in England with nothing to do that does it so gracefully and is so bland and dignified and comely. But when I say that Bath does nothing I mean only in comparison with what are called industrial towns, such as her neighbour Bristol. As a matter of fact, she does much, for in addition to having given us excellent biscuits since 1735, and since I know not when the sweet and sticky buns that are named after her, she cures the sick, strengthens the lame, and provides the most distinguished surroundings for those who prefer repose to activity: in fact, I can think of no more attractive haven in which to moor one's battered old hulk for the evening of life.

A peculiarity of Bath is that she is of both past and present; for even where she is very old, as in the Roman section of her health establishment, she may be said also to be new, since with the expenditure of a little money and a few weeks' work this Roman installation, so carefully built and arranged all those centuries ago, could be put into use again. As it is, it is a show; but it could easily function, and then Bath would be even more popular than it is, for there would be added allurement to the visitor if he could feel like a proud and powerful centurion, aquiline and insolent, luxuriating in the tepid water as he enjoyed a well-earned rest from conquering Britain and—probably a harder task—governing its inhabitants. Even as it is, one can without much difficulty visualize him at his relaxation; but it is not so simple to reconstruct the old busy Forum in the space between the Abbey and the Pump Room Hotel where to-day the bath-chairmen wait for custom: the bath-chair, of course, being as indigenous as the Bath bun, only having lost its capital letter.

According to legend, the Romans did not discover the special curative properties of the Bath springs, but merely developed them. The story goes that their quality had long before been disclosed to that friend of man, the gentleman who pays the rent. In this way. Prince Bladud, before he became King Bladud, a British monarch and the father of King Lear, contracted leprosy, and while seeking his living as an outcast worked as a Somersetshire swine-herd. The animals in his charge were infected, too, but were always the better, he observed, after wallowing in the marshy meadows at Keynsham, where the waters of Bath have their beginnings. Following the example of the pigs, Bladud also wallowed, was healed, resumed his status at court, and spread the glad tidings.

For our purpose, however, the Bath waters were first systematically put to their beneficent work by the invaders from Italy in the first century A.D. Subsequently, I might remark, King Bladud became the first British aviator, but failed as dismally, and very much in the same way, as Icarus—thus leaving the throne vacant for Shakespeare's most tragic figure.

Having only half a bishop, Bath has no cathedral; the Somersetshire cathedral city is Wells, which claims the other moiety of his spiritual lordship. But Bath Abbey is not therefore to be treated too lightly, for it has fine glass and interesting sculpture and some famous tombs, and as a building in the Late Perpendicular style it ranks high. Before the present structure, which dates from the fifteenth century, there was a Norman church here, and a Saxon. The story of the origin of Bath Abbey more or less as we know it, and of the representation of Jacob's Ladder on the west' front, has peculiar symmetry. In the days when Bath had the Bishop all to itself—for it did not share the see with Wells until comparatively recently—one of the line was named Oliver King, who, in 1495, dreamed a dream wherein he saw a ladder on which angels ascended

and descended, and heard a voice crying: 'Let an
olive establish the crown, and let a *king* restore the
Church.' To a bishop named Oliver King, with
ecclesiastical riches at his back, the path of duty was,
after such a sign, plain, and the Abbey was begun.
But before it could be finished, in 1509, there were
many vicissitudes in store, including the vandalism
of the Reformation.

The Bishop's dream was translated into stone on
the Abbey's west front, and the two ladders are still
to be seen, but the angels have suffered sadly and
are but shapeless lumps. Within, there is fine
accommodation for glass, but the glass is not notable.
Among the memorials is that of James Quin, the
comedian, with a bust and Garrick's lines, and I like
also the relief on the tomb of James Grieve, physician
to Elizabeth, Empress of Russia, where we see a
venerable student being approached by Death and
Time, whom a female figure, representing, I should
guess, Science, attempts to repulse. Another excellent relief is that of a gentleman with a handful of
flowers: John Sibthorp, a local botanist.

To Beau Nash is usually given the credit for the
rise of Bath, but he had a predecessor: Tobias
Venner (1577–1660), the physician, who (after the
Romans) was the real creator of its medicinal fame.
Nash merely imposed frivolity. Venner, by the
way, not only extolled the virtues of Bath waters

BATH
THE ABBEY AND THE ROMAN BATHS

but deplored the prevalence of smoking. As long ago as 1621 he published a treatise against the weed, wherein he attacked all smokers and particularly those who smoked as they walked and those who smoked between the courses at meals: an effort that would appear to have been in vain.

The first great event in the history of Bath's popularity, to which Venner's words and practice had so much contributed, was the visit of Queen Anne in 1703. Beau Nash, who in that year was twenty-nine, and who arrived in Bath in 1704, had been bred as a barrister and was already famous in London for his courage as a gambler, for his wit, and for a kind of general efficiency such as he displayed when he produced the Middle Temple pageant in 1695. Finding everything in Bath that the idle rich and the gouty could require, but all without direction or co-ordination, he set himself to farm it, and succeeded so well that he became as autocratic and as wealthy as he could desire, and Bath drew all fashionable and foppish people not only from London, but from the country at large, and even from abroad. Until 1740, when Parliament began a vigilant campaign against gambling, Nash prospered; but from this point his fortunes waned, and he died, in 1761, a poor and discredited man, aged eighty-seven. His tomb is in Bath Abbey.

In his prime Nash was a king. He drove in a

chariot drawn by six grey horses, with outriders and footmen. He wore an immense cream-coloured beaver hat, such as (his own reason for it) no thief would be able to steal without embarrassment; he built the Assembly Rooms and drew up a code of conduct for them which no one, not even a Royal visitor, might contravene. One thinks of a beau, and particularly of so renowned a beau, as a man of considerable height, grace, and good looks. But the full-length figure of Nash, in the Pump Room, shows him to have been plain, short and stocky. Apart from memorials such as this, his fame in Bath is kept alive by a cinema theatre named after him.

Nash put Bath on the map, as we say, but his interest in the place was mercenary. If there had been a strict law against gambling he would have settled elsewhere. The true father of the beautiful city of Bath which we know and admire and return to was Ralph Allen (1694–1764), who from humble beginnings grew to great wealth, partly by improving England's postal service and taking a commission on it, and partly by acquiring the local quarries and promoting buildings of stone. You may see his town house on North Parade; you may see on the hills in the east Sham Castle, as it is called, a mediaeval framework which he set there to improve his own prospect. Perhaps the best view of it is along North Parade Passage (where Sally Lunn's little shop with its bow window is still to be seen), where it completes the vista. Allen, who for his country residence built the mansion in Prior Park which is now a Roman Catholic School, and which every one should see for its lovely little Palladian bridge, was something more than a far-sighted benevolent municipalist; he was the friend of Fielding, who wrote much of *Tom Jones* in Bath at Widcombe Lodge, and is thought to have based Squire Allworthy upon him; he was the friend of Pope, who found in his kindly, modest, charitable ways the inspiration for the line:

'Do good by stealth and blush to find it fame';

he was the friend of Pitt.

But Allen would not have been able to make this new and distinguished resort without the help of his two architects, John Wood the elder and John Wood the younger, to whom most of the houses of the great period, the middle of the eighteenth century, are due.

If there is any purely residential architectural scheme anywhere in England as bold and successful as Royal Crescent, I have not seen it. A series of the finest urban abodes out of the West-end of London, it has a quality of its own, changing but alluring, all the year round, and it is fitting that that

sturdy Man of Letters and Man of Taste, George
Saintsbury, should have made his home there and
died there, the other day, at the age of eighty-seven.
I was there last on a hot morning in early summer
when the city below was basking in a haze.   The
sun was held and reflected by this extended arc
made splendid by its Ionic pillars.   Again I realized
how foreign Bath is, and when a milkman passed
with his two pails on a yoke, I realized also how
much of yesterday it still preserves.   In the meadow
below the ha-ha of the Crescent garden four black
funeral horses, with nothing else to do, frolicked
like two-year-olds in the long grass: a reassuring
testimony to the salubrity of the place.

Bath is not only a drone herself, but makes drones
of her guests, who in the business of idling can get
through the day amusingly enough.   I, personally,
like to lean over the North Parade bridge, to watch
the rapid Avon flowing below it and to see the lovely
Pulteney bridge, with its three perfect arches: a
bridge which, when you are upon it, is not a bridge
at all, but a section of a narrow street of shops.   It
is from the other side of the North Parade bridge
that you see the Grotto, now derelict in a private
garden, which once was famous as the resort of
lovers, among them Richard Brinsley Sheridan and
the beautiful Elizabeth Linley, whom he courted
here in 1770 and subsequently eloped with and

married. One of the Bath picture-postcards repro-
duces a four-lined verse, in the stilted manner of the
time, which the future author of *The School for
Scandal* addressed to the lovely girl:

'Uncouth is this moss-covered Grotto of stone,
    And damp is the shade of this dew-dripping tree;
Yet I this rude Grotto with rapture will own,
    And, Willow, thy damps are refreshing to me.'

Sheridan, who lived both at Londonderry House
and at 7, Terrace Walk, where he wrote *The Rivals*,
has an hotel named after him. The Linleys lived at
1, Orchard Street. But if I were to begin seriously
to name all the famous residents I should require
endless pages. Enough that there are many tablets,
and not the least exciting thing for the visitor to
Bath to do is to hunt for them on these blackening
façades—not black, as London stone fronts are,
from soot, but from some inherent discolouring
constituent. North Parade alone yields good sport:
Wordsworth lodged at No. 9; Goldsmith at No. 11.
At No. 6, South Parade, Walter Scott stayed when
a child with his uncle.

Perhaps the most distinguished of all Bath's great
men is Thomas Gainsborough, the portrait-painter,
who settled here in 1760, when he was thirty-three,
taking rooms in the house now named after him
near the Abbey, and afterwards at No. 24, the

Circus, where he remained until, some twelve years later, he decided to attack the capital itself, and to become an even closer rival of Sir Joshua Reynolds. At Bath he painted some of his finest things, and the fact that his studio was in this town made it necessary for many persons of eminence who wished to be limned by him to visit it, whether they otherwise wanted to or not.

After Gainsborough Bath's most fashionable painter was the youthful Lawrence, later Sir Thomas Lawrence, P.R.A., whose precocious pencil was the wonder of so many travellers who stopped at the Bear Inn at Devizes, of which the boy's father was landlord. The young Lawrence's studio, at 2, Alfred Place, was thronged until, like Gainsborough, he found the call of London irresistible.

The rather obvious work of Bath's own special painter, Thomas Barker, or 'Barker of Bath', may be studied in the Victoria Art Gallery; but the effort will not be too richly repaid. During his life he was known almost solely by 'The Woodman', a picture which was much engraved and which Miss Linwood executed in wool-work. If you do not see her actual reproduction in any of Bath's myriad antique shops, you will find many like it.

The Victoria Art Gallery has little that is of the first class, but more than once I have loitered there very pleasantly. You will find there a pencil draw-

ing of Elizabeth Linley by Sir Joshua; a large river
scene—a fishing party—by Joseph Farington, whose
diaries not long ago were discovered and published;
and an interesting selection of modern water-colours
ranging from Prout to Brabazon, from Alfred Par-
sons to A. D. Innes.   And the Bath stocks are here,
too, in which misbehaviourists were ignominiously
placed, to be mocked at, if not actually pelted, by
those fortunate enough to have the right to pass
judgment.

Bath's other formal Art Gallery, the Holbourne
Museum, is more remarkable for its silver than its
paint, and one comes sadly to the conclusion that
the original collector of these dubious canvases was
the dealers' best friend.   There are also, in the
Pump Room, a number of very interesting Somersetshire landscapes, in water-colour, by Samuel
Poole.   But one does not go to Bath to see pictures
or silver or curiosities; the appeal of Bath is Bath:
a distinguished city of leisure and repose and health-
giving and hope-giving springs.

Passing slowly past the discreet Royal Crescent
houses, so solid, so comfortable, I always wonder
which was the door that blew to on the cold night
when Mrs. Dowler returned in a Sedan-chair and
Mr. Winkle rashly went down to let her in.   At
No. 5 lived Christopher Anstey, the satirist, whose
volume of light verse, called *The New Bath Guide*,

made him famous and Bath even more famous, and won him, in less critical and exacting days than these, a resting-place in Poets' Corner, Westminster Abbey.

I am not sure that Bath's most considerable gift to the world was not Mr. Moses Pickwick, the proprietor of the coaches between Bath and London, who, it is thought, provided Dickens with the immortal name. It will be recalled by the devout that when Sam Weller descried the name of this worthy and useful citizen on the door of the vehicle, all his loyalties were roused and he boiled with indignation. 'I'm wery much afeerd, Sir,' said Sam to his master, 'that the proprieator o' this here coach is a playin' some imperence with us. And that ain't all,' he continued: 'not content with writin' up Pickwick, they puts "Moses" afore it, vich I call addin' insult to injury, as the parrot said ven they not only took him from his native land but made him talk the English langwidge arterwards. . . . Ain't nobody to be whopped?'

History relates that, owing to the comic associations which steadily gathered around his name, Mr. Moses Pickwick became as hostile to it as Sam Weller had been, and actually changed it. From Pickwick he became Sainsbury, a name which, wherever you are in Bath to-day, is strongly evident; but Mr. H. V. Morton, when he was here not long ago in the process of 'searching England', found and talked with an actual Mr. Pickwick.

According to a picture-postcard, Dickens stayed at the Saracen's Head in Broad Street, but he was also a visitor at No. 35, St. James's Square, where Walter Savage Landor, whom he portrayed so lovingly as Leonard Boythorn in *Bleak House*, lived. Thackeray was for a while at No. 5, the Circus. We find Bath also in the background of two stories by an immediate predecessor of Dickens—in *Northanger Abbey* and in *Persuasion*, by Jane Austen, who lived at 4, Sydney Place, from 1801 to 1805. Admiral Croft, that pleasant old sea dog in the later book, put the case for Bath very comprehensively. 'It suits us very well,' he said. 'We are always meeting with some old friend or other; the streets full of them every morning; sure to have plenty of that; and then we get away from them all, and shut ourselves in our lodgings, and draw in our chairs, and are as snug as if we were at home.'

The Admiral might have gone on to say something of his gout and the alleviation he was obtaining, for, of course, he had gout and, of course, Bath was doing it good. And were he speaking now he would say something of the beauty of the Botanic Garden in Victoria Park, where one finds the most exquisite plants and trees and flowers, and where one of the springs of the Romans' Aquæ Sulis rises. A little

11

temple marks the spot, while behind this temple, across the way, just beneath the Via Julia, the Roman road, is a great head of Jupiter rising from a tangle of ivy, contemplating the valley. I hoped that this was a relic excavated from the soil, but I find it is the work of a modern local sculptor.

To return to Miss Austen's Admiral, he would be just as happy in Bath to-day drinking his three glasses of water in the Institution Gardens (which is not really as like warm flat-irons as Sam Weller found it), sitting on a Sheraton chair in the Pump Room reading the papers brought to him by liveried servants, and at tea-time eating a Bath bun in Green Street or Milsom Street. Very little that is changed would he see; in fact, nothing but motor-cars in place of carriages and gigs, and (in spite of old Tobias Venner, the Bath physician), cigarettes in every mouth, even those of women and girls.

OLD ENGLISH LANDMARKS

A RECENT annual report of that most necessary board of vigilance, the Society for the
Protection of Ancient Buildings (founded by
the author of *The Earthly Paradise* in 1877) was made
important and memorable by an address by a stalwart
friend of the best causes, Mr. D. S. MacColl, whose
keen eye and sure and uncompromising pen are a
national asset. One of Mr. MacColl's suggestions,
which struck me as being sound as well as imaginative,
was to preserve some of our old barns by converting
them into hostels for hikers. 'If it were left to me,'
he added, 'if, unhappily, a vote had to be taken
between the loss of ancient churches and ancient
barns—I confess that very often my vote would be
for the barns. For one reason, they have a fine
simplicity not only of structure, but of illumina-
tion you do not get in the church, where very often
there is an awkward conflict of lights. The
mysterious welling of light among the old beams
and timbers of a barn is one of the loveliest things
upon earth.'

That sentence touches several spots. It sends

the mind to paintings by Sir George Clausen and
etchings by Mr. Muirhead Bone, and to certain
barns which I can evoke at any moment, such as
the great church barn at Bradford-on-Avon, and
another great ecclesiastical barn just under Bredon
Hill, and a secular barn at Alciston in Sussex,
where 'the mysterious welling of light' is at
its most gracious, and many other less imposing
barns on farms all over the country, at once unpretentious but grand and impressive. Our wooden
ships, which are outside the scope of this Society,
fall to pieces almost daily; but the inverted hulls of
the land—the roofs of barns—with their beams and
timbers and joists and undulating lines, need never
be allowed to decay.

So important are they that there might even be a
special derivative society formed to care for them
—the Society for the Protection of Barns—part of
whose duty would be to see that the younger men
were brought up with a knowledge of the art of
thatching. 'Is your son a thatcher too?' I once
asked an elderly Berkshire labourer at work on a
roof. 'No,' he said, 'not he: he's a clerk in Reading.'
I put a similar question the other day to a Kentish
shearer. 'Can your son shear?' I asked him. 'He
shear?' he replied in amazement. 'He'd despise
it; he's in a garage.' How then will the barns be
re-thatched? They won't be; they will either be

left to rot, or that foulest invention of mechanical purblind man, galvanized iron, will be spread over them. And our sheep will be shorn by machinery and another link with the honourable and solicitous past be broken.

Every year in the early spring I go to Romney Marsh to see the lambs scattered about the green levels, falling—as they and their mothers always do —into perfect composition; and every year, later, I go again to see the shearing. For electricity has not yet made its way there. Nor has it yet generally invaded the cow-house, although I saw, for the first time, not long since, in Sussex, the process of milking by electricity and was duly saddened. For if there is electricity there will no longer be any milking stool, any pail (the milk being conveyed through pipes to some distant spot) and, far more deplorable, there will no longer be any milkmaid. What thus becomes of Sir Thomas Overbury's beautiful 'Character' of one of them? What thus becomes of Austin Dobson's gay new song to an old tune?

> 'Across the grass I see her pass;
>   She comes with tripping pace,—
> A maid I know,—and March winds blow
>   Her hair across her face.
>   With a hey, Dolly! ho, Dolly!
>   Dolly shall be mine,
>   Before the spray is white with May,
>   Or blooms the eglantine.'

—That is how the Dobson poem begins; and thus
it goes on:

'Let those who will be proud and chill.
For me, from June to June,
My Dolly's words are sweet as curds—
Her laugh is like a tune.
With a hey, Dolly! ho, Dolly!
Dolly shall be mine,
Before the spray is white with May,
Or blooms the eglantine.'

And here is Sir Thomas's tribute: 'All her excel-
lencies stand in her so silently, as if they had stolen
upon her without her knowledge. The lining of
her apparel (which is herself) is far better than out-
sides of tissue; for though she be not arrayed in the
spoil of the silkworm, she is decked in innocency,
a far better wearing. She doth not, with lying long
a-bed, spoil both her complexion and conditions;
nature hath taught her too immoderate sleep is rust
to the soul; she rises therefore with chanticleer, her
dame's cock, and at night makes lamb her curfew.
. . . She makes her hand hard with labour, and
her heart soft with pity; and when winter's evenings
fall early, (sitting at her merry wheel) she sings a
defiance to the giddy wheel of fortune. She doth
all things with so sweet a grace, it seems ignorance
will not suffer her to do ill, because her mind is to
do well. She bestows her year's wages at next fair:

and, in choosing her garments, counts no bravery in the world like decency.   The garden and beehive are all her physic and chirurgery, and she lives the longer for it.   She dares go alone and unfold sheep in the night, and fears no manner of ill because she means none; yet, to say truth, she is never alone, for she is still accompanied with old songs, honest thoughts, and prayers, but short ones. . . .   Thus lives she, and all her care is that she may die in the spring-time, to have store of flowers stuck upon her winding-sheet.'

Finally, to come to the actual task now being removed from her for ever: 'In milking a cow and straining the teats through her fingers, it seems that so sweet a milk-press makes the milk the sweeter or whiter; for never came almond glove or aromatic ointment off her palm to taint it.'

What has electricity to offer in exchange for this?

But if there is not yet a special branch for barns, the Society has just appointed a committee to look after our windmills. I am delighted, said Mr. MacColl, to see 'there is to be a Secretary for Windmills, and a Special Committee. Why do windmills excite our admiration and affection as a power-station does not? Surely for this reason, that their means of action are not invisible. We can actually see and trace the human contrivance in conjunction with the force of Nature. The windmill is practically an anchored ship. It is not so beautiful as a ship, which yields more freely in its rhythms to the action of winds and waves, but it shares something of that beauty in the way the wind acts upon it. The steam-trawler and the motor launch are a poor exchange in beauty for the fishing-smack and the sail- or horse-driven barge of which our coasts and rivers and canals are being stripped. And that is so all through. There is necessarily much more beauty as well as humanity where you can see how things work than when you see a shape going through the water or along the road in which the means of propulsion are concealed or semi-concealed. The aeroplane is a betwixt and between: it looks like, without being, a bird'.

Whether the Society intended merely to preserve windmills or to set them going again, I am not informed. Probably merely to preserve, although I read that by its aid the miller of Haverhill in Suffolk was enabled to resume work. But even if they grind nothing, the sails might go round. 'There are', said one of the most zestful and observant writers that England has ever had, 'few merrier spectacles than that of many windmills bickering together in a fresh breeze over a woody country; their halting alacrity of movement, their pleasant business, making bread all day with uncouth gesticulations, their air, gigantically human, as of a creature half alive, put a spirit of romance into the tamest landscape.' So wrote Stevenson, and every one must agree with him, except perhaps those millers who grind by steam. But the chivalrous, melancholy Spanish redresser of wrongs would not be utterly lost if he found himself, on his sorry nag Rosinante, in England to-day. Near Ashford is a white windmill which is constantly in action, and there is another at Westenhanger, to cheer the eyes of all who use the London-Folkestone road, and one at Blackboys in Sussex, and another near Ditchling, although the two on the downs facing that village have long been nothing but idle landmarks. No doubt there are many more, but these are the only ones that I have seen recently, to which must be added the windmill at Rye just rebuilt. In a quiescent state are a far greater number, some cared for and some left as forlorn relics: such as that deplorable object near Hurstmonceux, with the rust on it, and a neighbour at Ninfield, with only two sails or sweeps left. This tendency to allow an inadequate number of sweeps to remain is deplorable. All or none.

Mr. MacColl is by no means hopeless, but his millennium is very different from that of the usual prophet of progress. The blessed future to which he looks forward is but a repetition of a remote past: the wheel is to come full circle. And the means by which this desirable end is to be reached is the over-population of this country due to the contracting of the rest of the world through the fact that all the other nations have 'learned the trick' of foreign exploitation. 'If', he says, 'with our redundant population, we get through at all, we shall be thrown back upon our own country and have to make it self-sufficient: something more like what is described in Mr. Trevelyan's History at the beginning of the reign of Queen Anne, when the natural waterways, the sea, the rivers and canals, carried so large a part of its traffic, and there was a national balance of life. We shall go back, when the coal and the petrol are exhausted, to the woods for fuel and the wind and water for power.' I personally shall not see this, but I shall lie no less quietly in the grave for the thought that such a state of things has come about.

A BEAUTIFIER OF ENGLAND

'GOD first planted a garden'; we know that, on the authority of Lord Bacon; but of the assiduity and methods of the first lady gardener we know little. I mean, as a lady gardener. What we do know is that on one occasion at least she disobeyed her Employer and lost her job. How long a step it is from Eve to the late Gertrude Jekyll no one can say: the evolutionist and the bishops are still at variance; but a long one, and it is odd that so few names of workers in their walk of life come between. But into the history of woman in horticulture I have not inquired too closely, being, in my own mind, satisfied with Miss Jekyll as the true pioneer.

Gertrude Jekyll was born in London on 29th November, 1843, so that at her lamented death on 8th December, 1932, she was very nearly ninety. She was the daughter of a soldier, and as a girl showed enough ability with pencil and brush to be trained for an artist, but her eyes beginning to be affected, she had to take to other interests. It is wonderful to think that any one with impaired sight was able to do so much towards increasing the visible beauty of her native land—for that was her life-work. One cannot sufficiently admire a victim of myopia who was an innovator in landscape-photography, in informal, but controlled, imaginative gardening, in rural architecture, and in the revival and nurture of domestic arts and crafts—for Miss Jekyll was an upholder of the hand against the machine, and her book on the old handicrafts of England is a classic.

Before Miss Jekyll there had been William Robinson, who lives in a grey Tudor manor house in Sussex, where, in the spring, aubretia tumbles over the stones in mauve and purple cascades. Mr. Robinson's great books, *The English Flower Garden* and *The Wild Garden*, laid emphasis on the importance of letting Nature have a hand in the disposition of plants; but it was left for Miss Jekyll, in her first book, *Wood and Garden*, published in 1899, to revolutionize the gardener's art and to kill the old stiff fashions of bedding. Since first books have a way of being the best, and are nearer the author's heart than any that follow, I take Miss Jekyll's credo from that: a credo which she has many times paraphrased, but never in more direct or better words:

'But the lesson I have thoroughly learnt, and wish to pass on to others, is to know the enduring happiness that the love of a garden gives. I rejoice when I see any one, and especially chil-

MISS GERTRUDE JEKYLL
From the Painting by William Nicholson in the Tate Gallery

dren, inquiring about flowers, and wanting gardens of their own, and carefully working in them.   For the love of gardening is a seed that, once sown, never dies, but always grows and grows to an enduring and ever-increasing source of happiness.

'If in the following chapters I have laid stress upon gardening for beautiful effect, it is because it is the way of gardening that I love best, and know most about, and that seems to me capable of giving the greatest amount of pleasure.   I am strongly for treating garden and wooded ground in a pictorial way mainly with large effects, and in the second place with lesser beautiful incidents, and for so arranging plants and trees and grassy spaces that they look happy and at home, and make no parade of conscious effort.   I try for beauty and harmony everywhere and especially for harmony of colour.   A garden so treated gives the delightful feeling of repose, and refreshment, and purest enjoyment of beauty, that seems to my understanding to be the best fulfilment of its purpose; while to the diligent worker its happiness is like the offering of a constant hymn of praise.   For I hold that the best purpose of a garden is to give delight and to give refreshment of mind, to soothe, to refine, and to lift up the heart in a spirit of praise and thankfulness.   It is certain that those who practise gardening in the best ways find it to be so.'

To-day much of that reads as though it were old-fashioned; but in 1899 it was to most people a novel doctrine.   How sound it was and how the light spread may be computed by the mere fact that, reading it now, you may wonder that it was worth while to quote it.   Such is the fate of innovators: they appear to be imitators, until a little research tells us that if they imitate any one, that one is themselves.

Here is a further confession:

'I do not envy the owners of very large gardens. The garden should fit its master or his tastes just as his clothes do; it should be neither too large nor too small, but just comfortable. If the garden is larger than he can individually govern and plan and look after, then he is no longer its master but its slave, just as surely as the much-too-rich man is the slave and not the master of his superfluous wealth. And when I hear of the great place with a kitchen garden of twenty acres within the walls, my heart sinks as I think of the uncomfortable disproportion between the man and those immediately around him, and his vast output of edible vegetation, and I fall to wondering how much of it goes as it should go, or whether the greater part of it does not go dribbling away, leaking into unholy back-channels; and of how the looking after it must needs be subdivided; and of how many side-interests are likely to steal in, and altogether how great a burden of anxiety or matter of temptation it must give rise to. A grand truth is in the old farmer's saying, "The master's eye makes the pig fat"; but how can any one master's eye fatten that vast pig of twenty acres, with all its minute and costly cultivation, its two or three crops a year off all ground given to soft vegetables, its stoves, pineries, figgeries, and all manner of glass structures?'

This book, *Wood and Garden*, not only contained such excellent passages of sweet reasonableness as I have quoted, but it was illustrated by the most beautiful photographs that, at that time, many of us had ever seen, all taken by the author. In fact, the book had the double effect of sending its readers out instantly to buy both a spade—or, at any rate, a Dutch hoe—and a camera.

In the days when her activity was great Miss Jekyll used to go all over the country to give advice as to the laying out of gardens, and her handiwork is everywhere to be seen—or the results of her handiwork, as observed by others and carried on. Hers was a peaceful, almost secret, revolution, the effects of which can never be effaced. But it was not only the rich who commanded her energy. Her heart was large enough to extend sympathy and helpfulness to every one with a genuine appeal; and this charming account of one of her minor commissions is a proof:

'Some of the most delightful of all gardens are the little strips in front of roadside cottages. They have a simple and tender charm that one may look for in vain in gardens of greater pretension. And the old garden flowers seem to know that there they are seen at their best; for where else can one see such Wallflowers, or Double Daisies, or White Rose bushes; such clustering masses of perennial Peas, or such well-kept flowery edgings of Pink, or Thrift, or London Pride?

'Among a good many calls for advice about laying out gardens, I remember an early one that was of special interest. It was the window-box of a factory lad in one of the great northern manufacturing towns. He had advertised in a mechanical paper that he wanted a tiny garden, as full of interest as might be, in a window-box; he knew nothing—would somebody help him with advice? So advice was sent and the box prepared. If I remember rightly the size was three feet by ten inches. A little later the post brought him little plants of mossy and silvery saxifrages, and a few small bulbs. Even some stones were sent, for it was to be a rock-garden, and there were to be two hills of different heights with rocky tops, and a longish valley with a sunny and a shady side.

'It was delightful to have the boy's letters full of keen interest and eager questions, and only difficult to restrain him from killing his plants with kindness, in the way of liberal doses of artificial manure. The very smallness of the tiny garden made each of its small features the more precious. I could picture his feeling of delightful anticipation when he saw the first little bluish blade of the Snowdrop patch pierce its mossy carpet. Would it, could it really grow into a real Snowdrop, with the modest, milk-white flower and the pretty green hearts on the outside of the inner petals, and the clear green stripes within? and would it really nod him a glad good-morning when he opened his window to greet it? And those few blunt reddish horny-looking snouts just coming through the ground, would they really grow into the brilliant blue of the early Squill, that would be like a bit of midsummer sky among the grimy surroundings of the attic window, and under that grey, soot-laden northern sky? I thought with pleasure how he would watch them in spare minutes of the dinner-hour spent at home, and think of them as he went forward and back to his work, and how the remembrance of the tender beauty of the full-blown flower would make him glad, and lift up his heart while "minding his mule" in the busy restless mill.'

—Is not that experience perfectly related? and does it not reveal a profoundly sincere character?

I find that, in the course of thirty years, I have dropped into my books three or four eulogies of Miss Jekyll, direct or oblique. They are too similar for all to be quoted here, but I should like to repeat the latest of them, in a 'conversational piece' called *The Barber's Clock*, published in 1931. It runs thus:

'My grandfather had a few roses,' said Richard, 'but geraniums, calceolarias and lobelias were his staple. Those were the regularized flowers of a gentleman's villa garden at that time, before Miss Jekyll had got to work with her revolutionary beautifying hand. No one person can so have transformed the face of England as the Lady of Munstead. Do you know her portrait at the Tate Gallery?'

'Yes,' said Jenny. 'So wise and comfortable.'

'And the portrait of her boots by the same painter,' said Richard. 'Have you seen that? The boots of one who loves the soil and understands it. I must get you a photograph.'

The photograph of the boots is not reproduced here, but I give the presentment of the shrewd, kindly, capable head that is so well known by all who go to the Millbank treasure-house. The one is the complement of the other: Mr. Nicholson, with nice insight, perceived that both extremes were needed.

The picture of the boots is a treasured possession of Sir Edwin Lutyens, R.A., England's most gifted architect, who, as a boy, had the advantage of seeing Miss Jekyll constantly and coming under the stimulating influence of her originality and taste. As every one in England knows, one of life's most prized possessions is a 'Lutyens house', and I am sure that Sir Edwin would be the first to admit that, but for his early companionship with

Miss Jekyll, Lutyens houses might not be quite the delectable things they are.   In fact, I find him writing in a number of *English Life*: 'It has been a matter of profound satisfaction for me to have been able here to pay even a passing tribute to this book [*Old English Household Life*] and to its author; not that I flatter myself I have thus discharged even in the smallest degree any of my great obligation to Miss Jekyll, her wisdom and encouragement, which has accumulated now over many years.'

It has given me great pleasure to write this further testimony to the glory of Gertrude Jekyll. I believe and say in all sobriety that next to the Creator no one has done so much as she to make England beautiful.

NOTE

The foregoing essays, all enlarged or amended for the purpose of this book, are reprinted, with permission, from *The Sunday Times*, *Country Life*, *The Strand Magazine*, *Nash's Magazine*, *The Cricketer* and *The Cornhill Magazine*.

I have to thank Mr. Bernard Darwin and Mr. Harvey Darton for improving the essay on 'The English Game', and Mrs. Fox Pitt and Mr. C. R. W. Nevinson for leave to reproduce the West Harnham sign board ; and my gratitude is due to Mr. E. T. Stotesbury, of Philadelphia, for the frontispiece from his Romney original.

E. V. L.

February, 1933